MARVINA SIMS

Copyright © 2022 by Marvina Sims.

No part of this book may be reproduced, stored in a retrieval system, or transmitted by any means, electronic, mechanical, photocopying, recording, or otherwise, without written permission from the author.

ISBN: 978-1-957009-41-4 (sc)
ISBN: 978-1-957009-42-1 (e)

Library of Congress Control Number: 2022903347

Introduction

When any of our senses first come into the realization of an object or entity, we attach a name to it. When we cannot name something, we look for descriptions. It's obvious that labels are required to identify everything in life. It's only when they are used to belittle another in hopes of reducing them to being less than someone or something else that these types of hurtful stigmas can mentally and emotionally cause damage to a person, sometimes lasting an entire lifetime. It's unfortunate that most people believe the terrible labels that have been bestowed upon them. Some, so much so that it causes them to have suicidal tendency, while too many have succeeded. If only more people could recognize sooner that those who use belittling labels only do it to make themselves feel better, which is why it is necessary for people to know that someone else's negative opinion should never matter—whether they are blood related or not.

In high school there was a guy who admired me and his way of expressing it was, "I just wish I could put you in my pocket and take you home with me." He went on to explain that I was so adorable to him that I resembled a Black barbie. That sort of adoration makes me feel warm inside just thinking about it today. And in case you're wondering no I never went home with him.

There was another time when I was in my early twenty's, walking around at a carnival, when I was still able to use crutches as a primary mobility aid, when a passerby yelled out, "What is that?" referencing me as if I was a monster or any non-human creature. My best friend, at the time, looked startled but then again, I got the impression that she was grinning and even enjoyed this stranger's banter of me. I acted as if I hadn't heard a thing but as I think of it today, I can still feel the sting.

Fast forward to a more recent occurrence, I was at the park with my daughter and granddaughter when a girl, who looked about twelve years old, walked up to me and said, "You are so pretty to me." I was pleasantly stunned because I was not expecting such a kind compliment from anyone, let alone a child. I still smile inside whenever it crosses my mind.

These scenarios are just a few of many where someone has outright labeled me. Regardless of when it occurred or what was said how I perceived each of them was on me. As a matter of fact, it is only my perception that really matters because that is what makes anything appear either better or worse, good or bad, horrible or great.

For instance, I will be a Black, female with a disability until my last breath on this earth. You who are reading this either felt a connection because of those labels. Or you were repulsed. Either way your judgement does not make my position good or bad. I am still who I am regardless of your sentiments. Remember, Les Brown said it best, "Someone's opinion of you does not have to become your reality."

God allows chaos   *giving us the option*

to wipe our canvas clean

It resembles a prison

an uncomfortable space

the only one

in a situation

becoming like new

to birth   *a new being!*

What parts of your life might God be molding for an improved image?

In Cahoots

It's so endearing
to not be left alone for nine months
straddled cozily in a womb
pulsing organs lull me
like an endless sound machine

suddenly
I'm out
unattached
screaming
shaking
in cool temperature

Mama's still here
waiting
with me
for me
even on me
my entire life

Abruptly she vanishes
no one replaces her
not even remotely

It feels like
everyone is intentionally treating me
in no way near how mama would
I then begin doing it to myself

Distancing from all that feels like
love
loving
or a replica among it

would fictional love do
I was given that on a silver platter
but rejected that too

NO LOVE is preferred
yeah
I'm much more comfortable with that

besides
everything I've ever acquainted with love
eventually fades
as if in cahoots with a vicious hurricane
can't stop it
can't catch it
can't contain it
undeliverable

tried ordering it
couldn't quite make out the menu
it's all so foreign

I end up preordering something
it makes me sick to the stomach
it looked prettier in the picture
I know what not to reorder next time

only next time it's a pseudo
funneling another inappropriate ingesting
I'm sick all over again
sick of hoping
I'm sick all over again
sick of wondering
sick of even trying anymore

I'll drink instead
it arrives
but that's no drink
It's salty tears
masked as a decorative salty rim
around a margarita glass

my mentioning this
gives this impression
that I care

I don't
I keep drinking
covering up
though failing to ebb the flow
no one will notice

I hope

The Black Father

The Black Father
was/is absent from too many homes
He did what was needed/necessary for him
Which actually turned out best for all
If we as adult children change the perspectives/narratives
in our hearts/minds
we may be able to drop the bitterness/blame/shame/anger/hurt
Drying up the tears is easier said than done
Cease the self-sabotage and go hard on hopes
where dreams no longer need deferring
What someone else did or did not do
Does not have to linger/end with you
Think about the help you need and get it
If it was in that bottle/drug/sex/food/gambling you'd be healed/over it by now
Ya think
It's in what you're telling yourself/believing
Again modify the opinions/feelings
Which would allow you a happily ever after
Quite often what you thought was the end
Can now be a new beginning
Even with the absenteeism
Of those we thought we needed!

Mom's Suicide Letter - March 1991

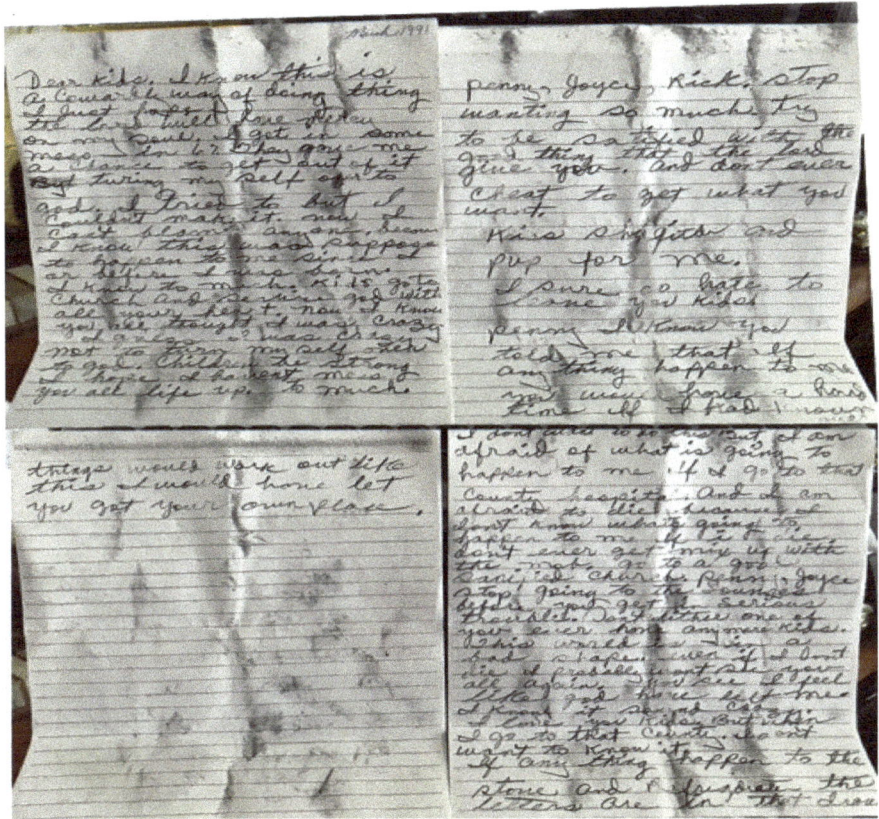

I held on to this letter because I knew there would someday come a time when I would want to use it for something. I didn't even consider myself a writer then, but I was certainly a collector. I'm pretty sure my subconscious already knew. Thankfully, Mom failed in yet another one of her suicide attempts.

I'm still in awe today because this letter is proof that loving moms never cease being loving moms even way after their children become adults and capable of caring for themselves. I had a chance to read this to a friend who said to me, "It's fascinating that the things we never think twice about someone who anticipates dying does." I took this to mean that my mom remembered to tell us where the warranty papers were in case the appliances malfunctioned, whereas those of us living tend to take functioning appliances for granted, and that would be the least of our concerns until they break down.

Mom passed away May 24, 2016—twenty-five years later—but not due to her own harm. She was residing in a nursing home because she was too feeble to care for herself. I am not at liberty to discuss the details of her death, due to a settlement agreement, but I believe I am allowed to say she supposedly/allegedly suffered a fall from her wheelchair, which supposedly/allegedly was the cause of her brain hemorrhage, a huge bump on her head, and a broken neck in two places, which then led to other body organs ceasing to function properly.

Thinking about my friend's statement today I am comforted knowing that my mom's desire to keep us properly nourished stems more from a selfless heart, though drowning in pain while still maintaining a nurturing spirit, than what I originally thought to be a guilty person's easy way out, attempting to redeem their selfishness.

I believe mental illness is one of the most difficult illnesses to handle, whether you're directly affected or it's affecting a loved one. I pray if this is you that you receive the needed help and maintain peace, love and continued understanding in the process.

FLOATING

take deep intentional breaths.

think about prioritizing one day at a time.

Non-Bodily Terms

I am so disproportionately crumpled. If I could stretch myself out to my full extent, it'll only worsen. The process of completing the task may take months or even years to accomplish, just one miniscule task, resulting in one humongous mess. It's a wonder I don't cause more problems in my current state. Pushing, pulling, pulling, pushing again…finally resting, then continuing the process. Sometimes this consistent procedure works to accomplish what is needed daily, or perhaps two or even three times daily. Sometimes it takes days or even weeks to complete. I don't mind the process but, in some instances, it causes undue hardship. It depends on the intake which determines the good or bad results of the output.

It's greed. That's exactly it. One of those good old seven deadly sins, creeping in…Again. I am told to resist the intake. But that's like telling the wolf of Wall Street to stop figuring out how to become richer. I can resist only for so long. Sometimes I can hold out for a few days, but the issue keeps returning like a fluttering moth to emitting flames of bonfires, even raging wild forest fires among darkness. Incapable of seeing any other way out so I take the worse route. "No! Don't do it! Fight it!" I figure if I keep trying to tune it out it'll keep…coming…back.

So, of course, once again I ignore those pesky old self-righteous voices that think they have the right to stifle what little options I have of creating self-fulfillment and happiness. Actually…it's only…one…voice…because the tone never changes but that one voice feels like many when you CAN'T…SHUT…IT…OFF!

I…have…experienced…
the…same…
horrific…outcome…
time…and…time…again.

It feels like severe self-punishment.

Perhaps this is my version of self-mutilation…or not.

I hear water helps but periodically it too does not live up
to its own standards—whatever those may be.

Leaf Me Alone

Thousands of Brown leaves snake along the concrete, trudging as if feet steps are swiftly kicking them. The rustling sound causes me to turn around. There are no other physical bodies present. I get the feeling they are. I just can't see them. I continue forward and see a leaf cross speedily in front of me. I wonder, how does it feel to be that one that got away? The bustling of a leaf entourage becomes annoying after five minutes of hearing it consistently.

Do other leaves hear each other, or are they only felt while connected at the limb? *The-one-that-got-away* ruminates in my brain…Continuously! At first, *the-one-that-got-away*, becomes a pleasant country and western song. Then, it is a bluesy tone, switching into a melodic R&B tune. It suddenly blares louder, becoming obnoxious, that headbanging type, from punk rock to a heavy metal monstrosity, electrifying incessantly. PLEASE STOP!

I have heard that you can take any song and turn it into gospel just by adding Jesus in there…somewhere… anywhere. But it does not work in this case, because if Jesus gets away, as that one did, WE ARE ALL FUCKED! RIGHT! It is only then that the thought of *that-one-that-got-away* stings. It's like I can hear it say, "Stop following me! Just leaf me alone!" in Dory's voice from the movie Finding Nemo. I follow it anyway—that one lonely looking leaf.

It seems to have a destination, as if working toward a lifelong goal. It stops abruptly, halted by a link in the chain link fence. The two Black spots on the leaf observe me, as if I'm their tower into freedom. When I look again, I notice a Dark, Brown, squiggly line, smirking at me.

I want to touch it to let it know it's not alone, it's safe, and that everything works out in its own way. So, I get closer to it, extend an arm to tap it with an assuring fingertip. But a sudden gust of wind snatches it and flings it into a parking lot. That one parked, isolated car, is unphased by the leaf sitting on top of its hood, giving the impression of a unique emblem, for an unheard-of make and model. How quickly that leaf has adjusted in its foreign environment. I have never experienced such envy in my life! It has no sense of what is expected of it: how it should be, who it should be, or even why it should be. Who wouldn't want to live like that—to just be… without expectations?

However, *that-one-that-got-away* does not remain in that state for long, as it is slightly pushed to the ground by another soft wind. It glides slowly at first, then picks up tremendous speed landing into the clamps of a bush. Thrown into different, undesirable twisted moments, directions, and emotional states. Not by self-will, or sequence of developments, but by an invincible divine dominance.

That Brown leaf stands out tremendously amongst all those Green leaves. But nary does that Brown leaf appear to be concerned….at least not in the public's eyes. That is until the Green leaves begin pushing, making waves, with the assistance of the wind that fiercely creates more pressure. Pressure…such a harmless word until others makes it so. Intense pressure. Mounting pressure. Unbearable pressure. Popular pressure on demand to remain homebound, on lockdown, to be, to do, to behave, to change, to stay the same, to transform into that most likable quality of Greenness, supple and firm, which is, actually not remote from the unpleasant crumbling of Dis-colored dryness, that moment where one appears to cause the most harm to another, the uninformed others, who have either witnessed or was taught that one tarnished Dis-colored leaf corrupts/infects all others.

I look closer into the bush and there are many other Brown leaves sitting, with their Dark patches, gazing at me sorrowfully…or is that the look of disdain? Being the empathetic, codependent-to-the-core, eager to please person I am, I feel their pain. I want to assist them out of it. I ask the wind to blow harder, but I am ignored. I jiggle the bush, but my efforts are moot. I give up as the prickly branches wound my skin. Now rendering us all helpless… again…trapped…isolated…humiliated…unsubstantiated…unappreciated…

    disassociated…

        mutilated…

            foliated…

                exuviated…

                      devaluated…

                        OBLITERATED

Those leaves left one massive Green tribe only to be encased by another, one just as callous as its previous village. I step back to ask that net-resembling bush: is freedom equivalent to isolation? Is isolation freedom? Isolated from harm yet free to feel safe? There is no response. Instead, I overhear:

It is okay little leaf to enjoy your final days

Crawling along concrete in zigzag sways

Stuck between branches as you lay

Excited to steer clear of the craze

Lunaticky to the point of outrage

Trapped in a walled-less cage

Sheathed in all ways

Isolation is a freedom kingdom

At least for some

W.O.R.K.

Is overrated
Exchange of misery for money
The federal mafia makes it so

It determines status
The higher paid the position
The more respect
The beliefs of the status stricken simple minded

"Respect should be earned"
Simply gives people another reason to hate
Upon meeting for the first time
Become acquainted
Then disapprove even more

Hate…due to jealousy or disdain
Asking and answering the mundane
"What do you do for a living"

Do they really care
Or simply need that awkward silence quieted

We should respect all bodies
Until we have reason not to
Not the other way 'round

Making a person earn respect
Simply confirms misery
Of those demanding it be that way

Work at something you love
After overcoming the shock of getting paid
Remain there
Now it's a career

Still call it work
The misery semi-diminishes
More satisfaction in laboring
Or is it

We would be just as happy
Doing whatever we desire

Paid laboring should also include:

- ✓ Mothering
- ✓ Fathering
- ✓ Reading/writing
- ✓ Cooking
- ✓ House cleaning
- ✓ Watching television
- ✓ Surfing the web
- ✓ Grocery shopping
- ✓ Texting/talking
- ✓ Lounging/meditating/resting

Still not enough of a necessity to receive recompence
Likened to that of hanging sloths
Volunteer Slavery

Now that enough has become miserable
Happiness becomes taboo
Work is anything that you *must* do to survive

Luxury is an eventual evil of regret and debt
The survivalistic provisions
Food

Clothes
Shelter
Transportation

But what's actually happening

Wear
Out
Re
Kindle

   Fatigue
Wear
Out
Re
Kindle

   Sickness
Wear
Out
Re
Kindle
   Doze…Eternally…

Merely to R.I.P.=Retire In Peace

F ORGET

U R

C ONCERNS

K EEP MINE

You

It

Him

Her

Them

Yall

Just-Us

It's not easy defining *Justice* when referencing *Just us*.
Lives are suffocated even when remaining *Just*
biking,
driving,
parking,
standing,
sitting,
jogging,
walking,
sleeping,
working,
laughing,
shopping,
responding,
conversing,
murmuring,
minding
our own business,
riding
the bus
or *Just* at home relaxing.

Black Lives Matter is a lot easier to say than to portray.
At least for those who are *Just* privileged that way.

All Lives Matter or at least they should.
But there is *Just* one type found strung up in woods.

Only one type of the non-guilty lives murdered by police.
Far too many *Just* going about their daily lives innocently.

Videos are displayed *Just* to entertain.
Societal's spectrum of emotions from tears of outrage

to cheers of WHOOO?RAAAY!

It's *Just* surreal to think that TOO MANY are not sad nor mad
But excitedly pleased and genuinely glad.

Another family member *Just* snuffed from earth.
Returned to how they were treated—dirt.

Lack of empathy toward beings of color
Just needs to desist.
Yet only the guilty evils are quick to anger and resist.

Police quit their jobs since they can no longer legally abuse and kill.
Nationally displaying that to *Just* serve and protect *ALL*
Is *Just* obviously against their will.

What's *Just* for generations to come?
Especially since what's viewed as *Justice* applies to everyone.
That is except it is *Just* NOT *Justice* for *Just us*!

Carib Golden Queen Tyson

Bingeing ReelBlack TV

Queen Cicely ebonizing the whitest of sets

Gracefully perfecting the craft

Puzzling viewers as to if racism really existed in 1956

Epitome of Black feminism—laidback and appearing carefree

Her first filmed role–*Carib Gold*

Too much went untold

Black and white seaman diving for bricks of gold

Then there's that one who overextends the greed

As if his desires are more important than any other's needs

A husband murdered on board and the thief escapes in silence

The honest seamen made to break the sad news to another's wife

Though scenes are poorly represented Cicely's tears appear sincere

Perhaps that's where all the real heartache was released

Satisfied witnessing the anguish despite knowing
the tastelessness in Black history

Cicely was repeatedly picked for various roles in film and photography

Exactly who and how did she get picked

Just like her mother I figured it was due to sucked dyks

And also like her mother I'm just another jealous bych.

**ALL HAIL QUEEN CICELY TYSON!
REST PEACEFULLY.**

Dead Plant, Breathing

Perhaps some of you need a brief description or three
Of the plant that knows how to burst through concrete
No longer feeling guilty for gifts
Which flows naturally
You've got to be able to trust yourself again
Prior to trusting those you call friends
Those who threw dirt in hopes of creating your end
Unaware that same soil only helped to revive you again

Surrounding and inborn negativity
- Anxious with anxiety
- Emotional beatings
- Verbal lashings
- Lonely barricades
- Drowning in depression
- Engaging in gossip, lies and backlashes

No need to resuscitate when you can selfatize
Drown in mental positivity
Water
Shine
Radiate
Nurture to nourish

Kindness dodges all desires
Though all desires have dissipated
Dead plant still breathing

Lingering Yet Vanished

Wiping falling tears as if it will cease the flow of more

Going/Gone Without Leaving
Leaving/Left Without Going
Lingering Yet Vanished

City mafia—mayor and cops
State and Federal mafias
The madness won't stop

Trickling down
and on
and on
and on
and on
and on
and on
and on
and on
MAKE IT STOP

Like a leaf blowing down the sidewalk accosted by grass

How easy it is for one lie to destroy an innocent person's Black azz.
Falsehood,
hoodwinked,
bamboozled,
wile.

This could take a while.
untruth,
tale,

fiction,
fabrication,
deceit,
dishonest,
deception,
trickery,
con,
fraud,
scam,
scheme,
swindle,
cheat,
trick,
fib,
sting,
ruse,
subterfuge,
All
For
The
Sake
Of
destruction

Three minorities
not separately
all in one
Black/disabled/(fe)male
Black/restricted/(wo)man
seen and unseen

Does knowledge help or hurt?
Lives still lost
My daughter your daughters,
my nephews your nephews
my uncle your uncles
my aunts your aunts

my cousins your cousins
My grand babies your grands
Every gender, race and age,
Cut off from the experience of a grandma, grandpa, neighbor, spouse, partner, lover, fiancés, other, they, her, he, she, them, stranger at the store, on the bus, in private and other unfamiliar public places echoing.

I now enjoy talking loudly just so those who I'm *not* talking to can hear me clearly 'cause I know they're *always* listening.

Someone is ALWAYS listening and watching and inquiring and desiring that free-spirited peaceful entity within me. Something this valuable is uneasy to retrieve or even maintain in this atmosphere/troposphere/ stratosphere.

Long years and har…I was about to say hard but it's more requiring of consistent and focused work. If it ain't metal, wood, granite, or hardened cement it ain't hard. The description is more like inconceivable to soak into any portion of the brain.

I'm ALWAYS educating.
You're welcome 'cause the pleasure is all mine.

Manic Pandemic

Those who survived feel as though they've aced it
Disgust consisting of amped
- levels of unethically paid aped politicians
- epic racial divide based on the color of the hide
- the loudest one to speak is beat down in the streets

you can never outrace what never dies
pecan skin is too far from pale
the cover becomes excessive kindness
or developing callous malice solidifying like ice
or bleeding like acid on an acne
calling it taking one for ALL like mine
feeling encased in a pane in an attempt to escape pain
damp and minced like an aged cap and ragged denim
in a twirling garbage disposal
encamped in a cinema of surreality
like a raped maiden
made to remain exposed
suffering the repeated malicious act
until the end of life
cunning ways to stall the medic
is merely an aide
in a mind panic
amid a manic pandemic

Post Pandemic Predictions April 23, 2020

It's September 2021. I watch my neighbor as she's yanking tomatoes from her yard, and turnip greens and more celery. How I wish I had the patience and know how to grow my own fruit and veggies. I want so badly to ask her how much she'll charge to make my yard look like a farm too. But I decide against it. I actually thought that since after the corona virus had everyone on lockdown and isolated so long that some of the evil ones would have a change of heart. Ha! It's back to normal for some people. As a matter of fact, there seems to be an increase of mass murders and bodies located in precarious places. The tension between the two of us is non-cordial as usual. We pretend we don't notice each other, when we're at a distance. And if we happen to be practically in each other's face we do a quick hand wave. But if we're driving past each other…Fawgitabawtit! No quick horn toot or wave. We totally ignore each other.

The only reason I'm watching her, out of her sight now, is to kill time. I've ordered my groceries and selected to pick it up at the store. It'll be ready in about half an hour. I kind of figured this is one of the things that would become mandatory after COVID-19. I need to get out for a few minutes since I've opted to remain homebound, even after the lockdown was rescinded. I had to listen to a lot of people complain about not being able to do fun outdoor activities, but it did not bother me at all, at least not as much as I thought it would. As a matter of fact, I welcomed that period of homebound rest. I think they should continue a period of a stay-at-home-month. Kind of like those unnecessary annual holidays, especially since crime supposedly went down and the air quality improved during national lockdown. As long as I had food, clean running water, wine, internet service and functioning other needed devices I was good.

It's too bad we must continue wearing these masks, or worse get vaccinated. I've never had the flu shot, because it made no sense to me to have a bacterium injected into you so that your body can build up its own immunity against a poison that someone else deems necessary for you to have. The fact that you can still get sick, after being vaccinated, really makes no sense. Why does the body need assistance with that? Like just because the Federal Drug Administration says it's good doesn't mean it is. They've been wrong before. Thankfully, I rarely get colds. I watched a doctor on a video who said that if you regularly put a few drops of peroxide into your ears, let it bubble up, until the bubbling slows down, then flush it out with warm water it helps ward off colds. It's funny because I was doing this due to earwax issues and didn't know I was helping my health in other ways. It's amazing how we get answers we're not even looking for. Anyway, I digress.

Back to the masks. I mean I am one who's all for using the imagination but it's not so fun when a dude is holding a conversation with you and he has a really nice sounding voice and a body like working out is what he lives for and I have to guess what he looks like. For instance, my car battery died, since I haven't driven it in a year. So, I called roadside services. Dude arrives thirty minutes later. He's buff in all the right places, has a smooth sounding voice. But then he takes the mask off and I'm like saying to myself put that shit back on, bro, please! Needless to say, my imagination was much more funner.

The other day, I decided to get out and join my family who had been planning to go to Six Flags since last year. Things are really weird now though because Six Flags has a strict capacity limit. They aren't allowed to ever get as crowded as it used to be. I understand the same restrictions are at all water parks and many other public places as well. Even standing in line requires staying back six feet still. They even make us sit two rows behind any riders we didn't come with. So, there are lots of empty seats. It's crazy. I'm sure eventually they'll reconstruct new seats, so it won't look so awkward. I'm standing in line watching all the empty seats, thinking I could have taken one and my daughter could've taken another. But during one roller coaster ride a group of twenty people were able to take up all the seats on a ride. But that's a rare occurrence. This new way of living is like something from a sci-fi book, or as I like to say, a sci-fact book.

EightING (-------(-)
Internal Navigation Guide)

Most refer to it as *reincarnation*. However, *that* word is much too simplified for such a complicated process. Yet, EightING-------(-) means aiding the soul. A powerful procedure that requires something extremely deeper than just body bouncing, demanding much action of additional description.

To jump, to bounce, to implant—EightING-------(-). It's a repeopling process of the soul. Resurfacing infinitively within various body types.

    Religioning can't control it-------(-)

      Pastoring cannot behold it -------(-)

        Choirs fail at singing about it-------(-)

          Humans are praying their souls keep it-------(-)

            Missionaries can't travel far enough to get it -------(-)

    Another attempt at hoping against hope gone awry.

Have you ever wondered, "Who laughs while dying?" Those who have never wandered to find out, "What the EightING -------(-) is happening?" They already comprehend. No longer *VERB*alizing desires;;; or mimicking biblical verses;;; or praying for a twist of miraculous events;;; or desiring longevity of living. It's a done deal. Though only with proper mating, can EightING-------(-) be enabled. Miniscule cells...are developing...completing...the structuring...in some cases...becoming...TOTALLY INCOMPLETE!

        -Not Seeing

-Not Crying

-Not Gurgling

-Not Feeling

-Not Murmuring

-Not Speaking

-Not Hearing

-Not Smelling

-Not Breathing

Likened to the aging…eventually…

EightING-------(-) means a new life begins…re-repeatedly…re-infinitely. EightING-------(-) another mound of flesh;;; subtracting another fleshly mound;;; Dis…solv…ing dust…i…ly. Then reviving again;;; continue Breathing;;; keep Interacting;;; enjoy Partying;;; Do-ing all the daily activities required in existing. Disconnection of worldly traditions.

RE-REDEMPTION EQUALS:

Self-killing and lying and stealing and cheating and hating and deceiving and manipulating and conning and physically beating and abandoning and robbing and killing another and inappropriately renaming and stereotyping and racializing and killing many and bullying and under-limiting (yourself and others) and controlling and believing evil is right and worshipping material items and lacking loving (for self and others).

EightING-------(-) is to begin again and again and again…within another… Living a new reality…for infinity.

NEED MORE CLARITY

how do I know when it's time to return / you begin preparing to transform when your chosen cell forms into a fetus / who decides my destination / you / what can I use to base my decision on / all pertinent data has been infused into the Karmputer / where might that be / Look within / You are currently the Eighter who will Karmp into the Eightee / look up; close your eyes; whatever you feel suctions you into the Eightee who's feeling the same / So focusing is pertinent / [Eighter does it] Oh no / I can't go into that Eightee / why not / the pain is unbearable / that's the point / your feight is to transform that / this is your only assignment / these are the stipulations:

                Jump into the EightING tunnel
                      Fall in as spirit
                    Knock up as flesh
                Kick around to get out
                    Pop out to join in
                    Be with the family
              Bring about drastic changes

                    - - - - - - -

In due time you:
    Pull out
        Pass away
            Leave behind
                      You either:
                            Go up
                                    go down

              But you can *NEVER* turn back around

                    - - - - - - -

what happens next / if you successfully change lives / in a positive way / you come back here / the process starts again with a different EightING prospect / if you mess up the assignment gets aborted / nearing your conclusion / the task goes awry / this song will start up in your head / replaying again and again / your moments of EightING ends / your soul is snatched downward:

*I want you here with me / come on inside my world / let me share my world with you / Be with me every day / I want you here with me / Cause you're so far away / I need you closer so I can fuck you / Fuck you in every way / Why don't you come on come on come on come to me / This is where you belong / So I can reject and fuck you / Fuck you the way I know you should be fucked / Since you feel the way I do pack your soul / I'm comin' to getchu / I need you by my side / when we're apart we're only **half alive** / Why don't you come on come on come on come to meee / And I wanna live I wanna live / Since you feel the way I do pack your soul / I'm comin' to getchuuuuuu / come on, come on, come on, come on, come on, come on, come to me / cooom to meee cooom to meee come to me / cooom to meee cooom to meee come to me*[1]

---

[1] Certain lyrics have been altered but is meant to be slowed and eerily sang based on the song by the O'Jays – *I Want You Here with Me*

Letter to My Younger Self

You are going to go through horrible heartaches. Your life is going to go from resembling the biblical character Job, who was extremely sick, his children passed away, his cherished possessions were taken away, and his wife turned against him, to being like Joseph, whose siblings lied on him and even tried to destroy and bury him alive, but he survived and became a rich ruler. Much of your hurt will be caused by the people you least expect by betrayal and lies to you and about you. In hindsight you'll realize that all of it was due to divine intervention. God needed certain people out of your life so that you can focus on being in your rightfully divine place life.

That's why Ma kept telling you that you were special. Had you seen it spiritually instead of physically you would not have gotten so upset. That's why you resisted it! But once you recognize that it is really known as "anointed favor" you'll receive it much better! Anything you'll ever desire will be yours! Just keep believing and watch how it keeps happening for you. Your mind is going to continue being blown based on miracle after miracle!

But way before that happens there will be a point where you will allow others to take you away from your true self. You will unfortunately relinquish your power to the man you marry because you'll believe that allowing him to lead is the answer to maintaining a happy marriage, as you were taught in the church. But the part you'll miss is that only works for men who reverence and submit to God. As a result, your marriage will fail, and you'll get divorced.

People will see your anointing and resent you for it because in their warped minds you make them look bad because you're doing better than them, especially since you're the one with the obvious disability. You'll begin noticing the jealousy in girls beginning in high school. This will continue throughout your adult life. You're not going to understand it because your self-esteem will be so shattered as a child by your abusive family members, so you won't see your greatness like everyone else can. But it works in your favor because it helps you to maintain humility. Your naivete of wanting the best for people and wanting to see them succeed will have you trusting wolves in sheep clothing, and believing they have your best interest at heart. You'll eventually learn that most of them are miserable themselves, so they hate to see you happy. As a result, they will try to sabotage you. This will confuse you because you won't be able to comprehend how your own flesh and blood and loved ones and relatives and people you grew up with could hate you so much when all you did was help them and wish the best for them.

Being able to see your awesome self is going to be extremely difficult for you because you were programmed as a child that how you feel doesn't matter. Even when you try to express yourself you will be mocked and belittled, rendering you to feel unimportant, invalidated and helpless. But you must learn to not give a fuck what anyone thinks of you. You'll master that eventually though. But in the meantime, you'll learn that all any of them narcissists desired was to use and abuse you to the point of bringing you to misery and self-loathing like themselves, in hopes of tearing your world apart. Once you learn that they enjoy seeing you hurt you'll wake up.

These evil spirited people will help you recognize a deeper meaning in the Bible scripture that says, "The thief cometh not, but for to steal, and to kill, and to destroy..." (John 10:10) You'll have stuff stolen from you materially, emotionally, and spiritually. The one thing that's going to shake your world is when your niece will bring a gun to your house to visit her brother, your nephew, in the middle of the night, while he's living in your basement. He's going to tell you how she pointed it at the ceiling aiming to shoot but he stops her. That same night God will show you the back of her head in your dream. You'll tell your nephew about your dream and that's when he will tell you what your niece did-confirming how she feels about you. You are also going to hear about the vicious gossip that'll be said about you from those same people you thought you were cool with, even your own brother and sister. All of this information will be difficult for you to process and will cause you so much grief and emotional turmoil because it will be extremely difficult for you to comprehend. Yeah, it'll be quite scary and devastating to learn that those who want to hurt and even kill you are your own blood. Yes. Those same people you go out of your way to help. But don't worry God will NOT allow you to be harmed by any of them bastards.

As a matter of fact, you will get empowered all over again! He'll open your eyes in time. You'll learn through various revelations and confirmations—through people keeping you informed and in dreams where God shows you the direction you need to take. But remember you must get to your lowest emotional darkness and despair before you begin to rebuild yourself again. But do not worry because whenever you're feeling you're at your breaking point He'll comfort you with clear visions and more dreams, which will soothe your worries about those loved ones who have passed away and any other concerns that distract you from peace. You'll even get earth angels who will give you the comfort and encouragement you'll need to press on at the exact time you need it. JUST HANG IN THERE. IT GETS BETTER.

All that pain from temporarily broken bones will not be any comparison to the soul wrenching hurt you will experience through heartaches. By the way, you are going to break your knees and your hip during your youth and again in adulthood. During those periods only certain ones are going to be there for you and it won't be those you call friends. Anyway, your life is going to get so excruciatingly depressing, to the point that you'll feel like you're losing your mind, and everything is pointless. You'll feel so alone, even with people around you, because they won't support or comfort you. As a matter of fact, it'll become quite clear to you whose enjoying your pain. People who stopped calling and coming around will start again when they see you becoming a come up. It is then that you must begin immediately cutting them off—going no contact or detached contact. You'll ace this though. Oh yeah, you'll have to create boundaries and tell them what you will no longer accept. They will continue disrespecting you and trying to show you they don't care about your new boundaries. They will even resent you for standing up for yourself. As a result, some will continue trying to agonize you while others will fall back, which is a good thing for you. Even though they will hate you even more for it, you will continue rising. When they see you being abundantly and exceedingly blessed beyond their comprehension, and even yours, by the way, some will try to be in your life again. DO NOT FALL FOR IT. MOVE ON AND ENJOY YOUR ABUNDANCE WITH THOSE WHO WERE WITH YOU THROUGH IT ALL.

Just hang in there, sometimes alone, and with the ones who sincerely love you, because it'll all be worth it! Eventually you'll see why so much pain and heartache was required! It was to build your character and make you wiser. Just remember only beautiful flowers can grow through dirt! And you are going to be that beautiful flower after all the dirt you grow throw.

So, brace yourself for the ugly and hold fast because eventually you will behold such a surreal level of inner beauty and peace, joy and happiness, that you will feel like you're already in heaven. You will learn what peace beyond understanding is like. You will learn what it feels like to love yourself like you tried to love others who didn't appreciate it. And the best part about it is you didn't think such a thing could exist for you. And what's even better no one can take any of that away from you no matter how much they hate and revolt against you! JUST HANG IN THERE. IT GETS BETTER.

The reason all of this will be an awesome experience in the end is because you'll have a phenomenal story to tell. One that will have so many believing that their miserable lives are worth hanging in there for too. And that's the most fulfilling feeling—to be able to help others realize they're not alone and it really does get better. Trust me on this one. You will be grateful those who were dead weight for you walked away and betrayed you. It will be like the trash took itself out. Just think, if they hadn't you would've never been clear minded enough to see they were merely your frenemies! I cannot stress this enough: JUST HANG IN THERE. IT DOES GETS BETTER.

You will finally realize why you never seemed to fit in with any of them and why you felt mediocrity was never for you. That's because deep down you always knew you were extraordinary: more like a Goddess Warrior Fucking Diva Queen! But you must lose the losers and learn to love your own company, because as long as you continue hanging with mediocre people it'll keep rubbing off on you. Stay away from messiness so you can continue to level up!

Much of what happens will teach you to trust people very little and trust God a whole lot more. These are all the reasons why you were introduced and accepted God at such a young age. Had this been any other way you would've lost your mind or even probably committed suicide. BUT God... Notice how He doesn't always expect you to listen for a small still voice with Him because He resonates quite clearly with you and through you.

Your faith will be your saving factor. Keep in mind that you are going to be so ridiculously blessed beyond measure and breaking those glass ceilings that all of them who turned against will come crawling back. But just remember that the hardships that you go through will all be so worth it. It's His way to prepare and strengthen you. So let all of this, from here on out, be confirmation enough for you to remember that you have absolutely ***NO REASON*** to ever fear anything else in life ever again—not even death! But of course, God's also gonna show you, in a very realistic dream, how peaceful that's gonna be for you too. Why do you think He speaks so clearly so you'd know it's His voice in order to understand His directions so well? Again, JUST HANG IN THERE. I PROMISE YOU IT GETS SO MUCH BETTER BECAUSE YOU ARE DEFINITLEY HIS CHOSEN ONE!

Angelic Whale

Massively beautiful
Diving from fog-like bellows
Flecking blue vapors from a turquoise bay

Journeying er'day
Twenty-five-hour watch
Hunt
Kill
Prey then pray
Or be haunted by the hunt
Praying about those who prey

Nourishment is the goal
Feeding the soul
Certain things told

No matter where she is on her voyage
She's in the proper place
At its proper time
Within the appropriate mind
Among every stratosphere
Strewn throughout millions of light-years

It was this time last year
No! Wait!
Try this time next year
No!
Try continuyears!
Incomprehensible to the so-so wo(man) kind.

The angelic whale
you thought referred to an outer entity
Try within the heart.

Bring It Up

I hope no one ever asks me
It was a botched job
They weren't supposed to hit the mother
She didn't do anything
It was her ratchet ass daughter
And grand kids
They were the target
Or at least one of them
Bringing the entire neighborhood into an uproar
It looked like a block party at first
Until someone showed their gun
Then it looked like a wild western in the hood
I was up
In case someone decided to randomly get trigger happy
I mean I don't really know who pulled the trigger
I do know who was associated with it
It was retaliatory
Aka by any means necessary
We dare not bring it up though
Some allude to it
In a roundabout way
But anyway, it felt justified
In hindsight it was vicious
Making the intent/motive moot
You can't just intentionally create aggravation
Without consequences
The cops suspected me as the ringleader at first
Following me around town
I go to a drive thru restaurant
There another one is
Penetratingly gazing at me
Hoping to intimidate me
But it doesn't work

I know they can't prove a damn thang
He takes his two fingers points at his eyes
Then directs them at me
I give him the finger
Then stick out my tongue
No, I don't really
But mentally it feels genuine
Now what I ponder on is
Since the murderer and the victim are both dead
Is it even worth writing about?

Continue Being God!

I see the sky as purple
With swirls of pink and turquoise
Streaks of yellow gold

I am
I am entitled
to improve God's creations

That's what giving Him the glory really means

I can make a house a home
My chair my throne
It's my imagination
Free to roam
Or to be left all alone

At first sight
Our fruits won't display
Vivid bee-and-bird attracting colors like
watermelon
apples
peaches
Or bananas

We strive to display
Goldeness
Goldenest
Godliness.
Above our best

More like a fight
Competing to outshine
Kindness
Cruelty lingers

Shy and quiet gets ignored
The bully takes the highlight
The real derivative of the squeaky wheel

The compliment is lost
Criticism persists
Lingering
Right there
Forty years strong
Much too long

A voice which should have peeled with youth.
CON – TIN – UES

A newborn
Remaining inborn
Never maturing
Mounting insensitivity
Nasty voices
The real reasons for so many bad choices

Caring too much
Insignificant things
Staggers growth
Too much power given to bullshyt

RELEASE

BREATHE

LIVE ANEW DAILY

CONTINUE BEING GOD!

Mere Experiments are the SPAB

I was already in bed but still not asleep when I got the call around 10ish. "Your mom fell out of her wheelchair at the dialysis center. She began complaining of a headache, so she was taken to Bill Tush Hospital in an ambulance." It was the nursing home…again.

My response, "She leaves dialysis at 8. Why are you just now calling me?"

"We were just informed and contacted you as soon we got the call," is the nurse's lame ass answer. I'm sure they knew much sooner than now.

Since this second-hand information is questionable, I call Bill Tush Hospital.

The emergency room rep explains, "We had her transferred to Tush Medical Center on Harrison Blvd. She was hemorrhaging on the brain, and we're not equipped to handle that here"

When I get to the hospital, mom is sleeping. Nothing about her looks injured to me.

The doctor is asking her questions. "Do you know what today is?" She responds correctly with her eyes still closed.

I ask, "Why won't she open her eyes?" The doctor says this is normal for an injured patient who suffers with diabetes and mental illness.

Even before becoming a resident at the nursing home, Mom had been committed somewhere too often, after refusing to take her meds. Each time she got committed, she would say, "They just want to experiment on my brain. I don't want them operating on my head." I tried constantly to convince her otherwise. Once she's better and home again I'd ask her if she remembered the stuff, she said and did, prior to being committed, but she never did.

The doctor continues asking mom questions. "Do you know where you are?" No response. "Do you know who the President of the United States is?"

"Obama." Mom says. Those were her last words for the following three weeks.

The doctor says they're gonna wait to see if the hemorrhaging stops on its own. I pray that they do not have to operate on her head, especially since she wasn't able to speak of these fears this time.

Hopefully, the outcome will be just as pleasant as the last two when she tried to overdose and again when she supposedly fell in her assistant living studio apartment. A rep at the facility claimed she fell and hit her head on the doorknob. Seems to me like they could've come up with a better lie than that. I believe someone cracked her skull open. She had to get 17 stitches on her scalp.

"But the doorknob is a lever that swivels up and down at the slightest touch," I report to an attorney. The only reason I even felt confident enough to talk to an attorney was because a doctor in the emergency room snitched. "Blood tests shows your mom has Seroquel in her system." I stare at her as though she'd transformed into my worst fear—a sinkhole. Seroquel causes her severe dizziness and even locked jaws. Well, this would explain why she really fell, if she really did.

"But she's allergic to Seroquel and they know this at the facility because on the spine of her chart it's written in bold blood-colored letters," I blurt out to the doctor. She looks at me as if she wants to say something more but walks away instead.

"Well now I've learned that the assisted living staff has been giving my mom Seroquel." I tell the same attorney, figuring now the bastardly medical staff at the senior home will get what's coming to them for trying to kill my mom. But none of this information convinced him we had a case. He said there's no way to prove any of what I'm telling him, especially since the emergency room doctor won't return my calls.

This is to be expected since I already know there's some sort of code of "misconduct" between attorneys and attorneys and doctors and doctors and doctors and attorneys. Apparently, my mom's case is one not worth breaking the code for, which is often the case for a SPAB. I told you I trust no one in the medical field and now I want to add certain attorneys to my distrust list.

I didn't just come to this conclusion, about doctors, from my mom's awful experiences but I found backup in books. After reading *Selling Sickness: How the World's Biggest Pharmaceutical Companies are Turning us into Patients* by Ray Moynihan and Alan Cassels, plus hearing various stories told to me by other people, I find it increasingly harder to believe anything medical professionals tell me. Even the author of the book says he was censored by the medical mafia and legalized drug lords. I'm paraphrasing but you know what I mean. They didn't want him to write anything at all, because educating the public equals fucking with *their* money. But enough is written to make those of us with a brain able to connect the sickening dots (some pun intended).

Thankfully *he* wasn't found dead due to some mysterious car accident like some of the research scientists who found the cure for cancer ended up. More stuff I watched in documentaries.

You should check out all of them as soon as you get a chance. It will blow your mind. Did you know the real reason the medical industry gets richer isn't because so many are sick but because of the fear they instill into those who may not even actually be sick? But worst of all, it's the *sick poor and Black* society who don't stand a chance of maintaining good health or recovering from illnesses, either due to no insurance, inappropriate insurance or just because they are too ignorant and poor to be able to know or even do better.

Anyway, after leaving the hospital that night I figured mom will sleep it off and be better in the morning. Not so. I get another call, from a medical staff claiming they needed my consent by phone to drain the blood from mom's hemorrhaging brain because it was starting to swell.

I return to the hospital to see my mom looking like a modern-day female Frankenstein experiment gone bad. Head shaved bald, both eyes swollen shut, a knot on top of her head, her face and body were bloated, it was as if they'd pumped fluids into her instead of sucking it out, a breathing tube was down her mouth and her twitches of discomfort made it all look even worse.

Since she remained alive through all that, they decided they needed to take her back into surgery. Her having a neck brace wasn't stabilizing her broken neck enough, which, by the way, was in two places. They wanted to operate to place pins in it so that it doesn't get worse.

So, I agreed figuring she'll pull through this too, as she's done with other crap she's gone through. But of course, when I asked them why they didn't do that when they took her into surgery the first time, they had some fraglenackle bullshit excuse. But I know the truth is they found another good reason to run up the bill.

God, I hope my family doesn't end up like most SPAB families. In the *Immortal Life of Henrietta Lacks*, by Rebecca Skloot, doctors and scientists never consulted the family as they stole and sold Mama Henrietta's cells and pocketed billions of dollars by using it to cure the world of various diseases. Those lying thieves didn't give the family a penny. Or similarly in the book, *Bad Blood: The Tuskegee Syphilis Experiment* by James H. Jones, where public health assholes lied just for the sake of learning more about how the disease affects SPABs. I saw the documentary of the Tuskegee Experiment. You really should check them all out.

Anyway, mom's damages seemed more like someone slammed her to the ground. I asked a nurse, "Have you ever seen anyone with these type of injuries from just falling from their chair?"

"No. I've seen damages like this from people who had fallen downstairs," she says. Finally, a response among the staff that feels sincere.

But the other nurse, little miss Cindy Brady look alike has this inappropriate minute grin, as if she's enjoying our pain. She comes in stating, "I want to assure you that we are doing all we can to get your mom better." What makes her statement more annoying than soothing is prior to her coming into the room I had just told my siblings that they may have made mom's injuries worse than they really were. This was just the beginning of several other conversations among us, which was brought up again only minutes later by doctors and nurses entering my mom's room. I'm convinced there's a camera somewhere.

So, I intentionally start saying derogatory shit that would have them coming in immediately afterwards, as if they expected me to wither like a water starved flower. They don't give a shit about saving mom. To them she's just another experiment on another old SPAB woman.

This time a doctor comes in repeating shit about my mom's health as if this same bullshit hasn't been discussed already. But what's different this time is he sounds as if he's churning back some bits of hostility. I avoid bursting up laughing in his face by shifting my attention to an inaudible television program. But then my brother, sister and I give each other glance over eyeballs and raised eyebrows as confirmation that these motherfuckers really are spying on us.

"Do you guys have a video camera in this room, or can you listen in on our conversation?" I blurt out to a nurse, who'd just walked in for the new shift. I was hoping to catch her up. She doesn't flinch as she responds with the straightest face any liar could ever convey, which is more deny and lie bullshit.

But they got me back for asking that question. "The only way your mom will be able to return to the nursing home is if she gets a trachea so that the nurses can keep her lungs clear of mucus so that she doesn't drown in her own fluids." The doctor says this as if he was asking if we needed our parking tickets validated. This new information hit my entire body like it was being defibrillated. There is no way my mom would want to live like a vegetable. Her exact words: "If I ever become a burden to yall, where I can't do nothin' for myself, just let me go."

"Since you're refusing the trachea there is nothing else that can be done for your mom at this point, we suggest taking her off life support." The doctor encourages. Now they're really pissed that I'm refusing to let them continue experimenting and running up the bill on this SPAB. My brother and sister agree with the doctor's suggestion a bit too quickly for me.

"I don't understand what's the rush. She's been through many bad injuries and pulled through them all," I tell them in the process of convincing myself.

"You have to take into consideration not just her injuries but her age now," is the doctor's response. Outwardly I'm silent. Inwardly I'm telling mom *you gots to prove them wrong, again.*

During the night I dream mom is limping, with a brace on one leg. It's like she's going through therapy. I believe strongly in my dreams. They are always a premonition for my real-life circumstances. I wake up and call my sister and brother. They both convince me that I'm just suffering from wishful thinking. Again, I feel defeated.

Every day I visit mom and remain from sunup to sundown. After a while me and various family members decide to take shifts. Since my niece went to visit mom one morning it freed me to go the Barber shop.

I'm sitting in the chair when my phone rings. It's my niece crying and frantically explaining, "I just walked in, and they are doing CPR on granny. I heard them call code blue as I was heading to her room, but I didn't think it was for her."

All I could think about is I refused to sign the Do Not Resuscitate documents so now more health issues are mysteriously occurring, requiring them to resuscitate her. Mom already told me, years back, that she did not want them pressing into her chest because she'd heard they break ribs doing it.

"I'm on my way," I tell my niece.

Now I'm finally convinced that this is a bigger battle than mom has ever dealt with. But once again I'm also convinced that they did something to cause her heart to stop. How convenient. Just as my niece was coming in.

Here again, I've seen a documentary where a mentally twisted nurse was giving patients medicine, which caused several of her patients' hearts to stop. The nurse was doing it for the mere enjoyment of resuscitating them.

I'm feeling even more helpless now because I know mom's heart did not stop on its own. But how and who's gonna help me prove that these doctors are the least bit interested in restoring my mom back to better health. They are ready to get rid of her now since they can't get me to agree to allow them to continue experimenting on her. So now more issues continue to conveniently occur.

I'm finally left alone with mom for longer than I've ever been since she's been here. I tell her, "Ma. You have to wake up…pleeeease. I miss us going shopping together. I got all the way to Walmart only to cry in the parking lot and ended up going back home because you weren't with me. I know you've suffered so much in life, but you've fought and won every battle. Please do it one more time just to prove these bastards wrong."

She opens her eyes wide, looking at me and says, "Heeeey!" The same words she yelled every time I, or anyone she loved, would visit her at the nursing home. But then she closes her eyes again and it was as if nothing happened. Were they controlling her mind with electrodes, like in those science fact movies? Now they're messing with me, wanting to make me look like the crazy one. God! Why couldn't I have been recording this!

I am so sorry mom that I was unable to stop them from experimenting on your brain as you always feared. But the rich, patriarchal, powers-that-be, has won again. Just as you predicted they would. Everything you said about them sounded like you were merely being paranoid, which is what they diagnosed you with, but now I know better. I sincerely hate that that was your last word to me and the last time I'll hear your nonrecorded voice again.

Bring Your Own Noose

Bad choices make fascinating

drama
      books
            exciting writings
                  movies
                        documentaries
                              local and national news
                                          gossip

The drug addicted mother is sentenced to prison
while the dead-beat dad, though convicted for attempted murder, roams free

An African American youth is publicly handcuffed
An innocent Black man and woman are murdered by the police
Yet none who are white are witnessed dealing with these same tragedies

A man physically harms a woman or child and may slightly get arrested
A woman hits a man and the public laughs at him
A child beats a parent, but it is the parent who is berated as bad

A white man hacks a system, robbing the economy of millions, and is labeled a genius then hired
A Black man who robs anything is labeled a thug and ostracized

Women are paid less but hired more
People with disabilities are paid less and hired less
All minorities remain the majority in lower paid employment

The LGBTQ+ community remains society's best kept dirty little secret
Hated by a society who uses God and the bible as their justification to hate

A silent conversation was recorded among some saying:
Oh, I know let's create a popular fiction novel for the world to read
We'll call it the *Declaration of Independence*
In hopes of convincing U.S. citizens that "all men are created equal"
Even make it appear that slavery is abolished, and segregation has ceased
All characters must remain subtle in their obvious hate
Label all murdered innocents and even hidden racism as a mistake
Since we can no long maintain the title of master
We'll create improved and beautiful disasters

Since they refuse to bring their own noose
We'll continue providing one for them.

SPAM

Spiced Ham
Shoulders of Pigs as Ham
Special Potted American Meal
More Like
Spackled Piece of Ass Meat
Jiggling and slithering within a metal barricade.
A glorious saving grace for the World War II brigade
The deprived man's potted steak
An impoverished nutritious meal on too many plates
All across America
The luxurious fucking United States!

No One Dares Mention

> "Get married," they say
> "Shacking up is not the best way"

Why marry the milk when the whole cow is free
At least…prior to the slaughtering spree
Both wallowing in bottomless pits of misery
    It begins by swearing best friends 'til the end
    Then someone goes and befriends another to append
        But…no one dares mention the probabilities of *that part*

Like a tiny spider descending a thin stringed web unseen
Dangling yet spiraling to and fro without wings
Hell breaks loose over mere minute things
    Screaming at one another about senselessness
    Yet wondering how it even got like this
        But…no one dares mention the probabilities of *that part*

Opting to heedlessly roam
Incompatible strangers in the same home
Destiny begs to amend a new end
Envy heightens toward those single friends
    Walk right by, avoiding contact of the eyes
    Wishing one another would just hurry up and die
        But…no one dares mention the probabilities of *that part*

Stepping over that thin line from love to hate
Ending the discussion with "it is best we separate"
Tear tracks become normalized
As so-called loved ones ostracize
        But…no one dares mention the probabilities of *that part*

Moving out is what one contemplates
Whelp! Too Late
The other has already sailed away
    Desiring to push PAUSE, REWIND, DELETE, STOP
    Stopping leads to another trip to the Apothecary Shoppe
        But…no one dares mention the probabilities of *that part*

            "How is your spouse" loathsome curiosity awakes
              The politically correct answer: "Oh just great"

But what one actually states:
    Loving that SOB has grown beyond hate
Already unmarried in a mental way
    After fifteen years abounds a life altering fate
Bedding in the kids' room for a peaceful lay
    In an attempt to avoid another excruciating headache

        Too   much   time   invested

        Another option   remain faux

Adulterated Adorations

    Arduous Arguments

        Counterfeit Concerns

            Careless Conversations

                Ersatz Emotions

                    Fraudulent Feelings

                      Hypocritical Happiness

                        Ludicrous Laughter

                          Shamming -Sex

                            Simulated Smiles

Yeeeah…But…no one dares mention the probabilities of *any* of *those parts*.

COSMOS = air + birthed + particles

Visualize air birthed particles of dusting stars hovering in darklight.
mentally + spiritually + psychologically + emotionally + cerebrally = divinely bountiful.
Galactic Journeys commence
miraculous observations + imaginations + speculations = unrequited explanations.
Essential incisive veracity necessitates
Spectacular arrangements of fauna resembling specks of fleshy anthropoid cyborgs.
Knowledgeable fragmented beings aging to return to their former habitat.
Internal universal islands longing for arrival though already home.
Star stuff of flesh is how the Cosmos recognize itself.
Shouldering biospheres of dreams + ecospheres of facts = Multimillion immense inceptions.
A fallen flawless snowflake + A biological dandelion seed = Conceptions of Immaculacy
Megacosms of blazing Stars = Outer Space disgorging!

Eternally Silenced

Birds singing so beautifully
Outside my kitchen window
A melodic rendition of gratitude
Successions of sporadic whistles
Chirps escaping multiple beaks
Some sounds outflow within the esophagus

The loudest continues
Cheep...cheep...cheep
Communicating
In her own language
Consistently
Rhythmically

Cheep...cheep...cheep
How nice it must be to stay in sync with yourself
Cheep...cheep...cheep
That preying dog
Growls
Barks BArks BARks BARks BARKS
Scratching the gate maniacally

But the cheeper isn't phased
Cheep...cheep...cheep

I look closer
There is a tiny puff of black feathers
A yellow streak along its back
Pressed into the corner
AN artificial protection from further harm
Unreachable
Helpless

Defenseless
Confused
Scared
No great way to continue living

No longer is this acoustic resembling beauty
More like a desperate plea
A blood curdling appeal to be nurtured and loved
Tearless
Ear-piercing plea
Pleading to be held
Touched
Stroked
Loved
Nursed back to health

Spilling into my spirit
Helplessness
Squeamishness
Timidity

I back up and spot its even tinier sibling
Inside my yard
Motionless
Swarmed with ants and flies
A position assisted by the dog

I go back inside
Pondering how to handle these
Uninvited
Useless
Critters of the ill fated

I go back out
There are now two motionless
Silent critters

Ceased singing beautifully
For me
For anyone
For ever

My worries fade
Like a loud engine driving away
I should be sad
I was sadder when it was crying out
Confirming my uselessness
Relief surges my soul
My burden made light
Silence makes me comfortable again

Sweeping them into a
Discarded
Dark
Empty
Box
Silenced
Eternally
Joining every soundless cell

FEAR OF PITCH BLACK

The real fear of pitch-black
Is equated with oxygen
The lights go out
Feels like your breath will stop…completely
Unable to see resembles suffocation
Even above dirt-
Rock, clay, organic matter, depending on the weather[1]
But above the clouds you breathe better
Oxygen feels purified
A swimming pool of fluff
Closer to the moon and sun
Is this where all the good spirits dwell?
Nothing moves
The pure act of just existing and being
Required to do nothing but be gorgeous like a kept wife
Now that doesn't seem like a bad thing
A kept cloud…where I want to be
My daughter once asked, "Is God on the biggest cloud?" I replied yes.
Years later I now get that question
To be even a goddess on a tiny cloud would be the highest honor
Ice crystals—bits of dust bonding together[2]
We're just specks with a vaporizable destiny
No sense in getting attached
Our own individual fate is just that
Borrowed ages, limited moments
In a distinct space
A belonging held only in the mind
Where your real heaven or hell dwells!

---

[1] www.garden.com
[2] www.nasa.gov

100-P Alley — Soul Food

I finally arrive at Coathang Street where BP Guest House, soul food restaurant is in Saigon. This joint is always crowded. I spot the owner and walk right past the line to greet him. "Hey! Hey! There's the man of every hour…Johnny Hill! I aint gotta ask whatchu know good 'cause I can already see you know a lotta good. Man, yo joint stays pipin' hot like fresh hot corn bread straight outta the oven!" We dap[1].

Johnny did damn good for himself. After serving ten years in the Vietnam war, he got with a beautiful Vietnamese woman, married her, and started his own soul food restaurant. I don't blame him for not goin' back to the U.S. There is too much chaos still goin' on with people fightin' over equal rights and it got even uglier after Dr. Martin Luther King was assassinated. I'm not lookin' forward to goin' back home to Alabama myself. Hell, I'm terrified even. Nothin' has changed with Blacks being lynched and not allowed to drink from any water fountain that doesn't say "coloreds only." I've heard too often how Blacks would survive war just to get back home and be killed by them racists honkies.

Word got out that Johnny's wife's name is the only one listed as the owner of the business. Even though some of the fellas tease him about it er'body know Johnny's the one runnin' this bitch. He had to do it that way 'cause even here they not lettin' a Black man own a thang.

It's like Johnny read my mind when he says, "Aaay…Jared, man, ya betta believe I worked my ass off fa all dis here." A worker says something to him. He quickly nods before turning his attention back to me. "Ya bout to eat in or just stopping by?"

"Maaan, aint no jus stoppin' by. When I'm in here I'm eatin' here."

"Cool. You aint gotta stand in that long ass line, man. Follow me."

Johnny takes me to a corner section to sit at a table for two. "Maaaan I sho appreciate this cause I'm hungry as hell," I tell him.

"Let me go grab you a menu." Seconds later he returns with a menu, a glass of water and an ash tray. "Ms. Ling Ling gonna be right over to take your order. It's good to see you again, Jared. Enjoy your meal and let me know if you need anything else."

I thank him as he walks away. All of it sounds so good. I wanna order er'thang on here. [2]

Authentic:	Piastres
Grilled T-Bone Steak	350
Kansas City Wrinkles (chitlins)	200
Bar-B-Q Ribs	190
Chopped Steak	180
Ham or Fried Pork Chops (Smoked of Fresh)	190
Breaded Veal Cutlet	180
Fresh Brook Trout (2)	190
Fried Chicken	170
Pigs Feet	175
Hog Maws	150
VEGETABLES	
Butter beans, rice with gravy, dressing, yellow yams, macaroni pie, collard greens, mustard and turnip greens, green peas, Black eyed peas, tomato salad, potato salad, corn on the cob, and cole slaw / corn bread and biscuits[2]	

After finally deciding what I wanted, I smoke a cigarette. Glancing over the room, I see how Johnny's makin' sure he can cram as many people in here as possible. The tables are so close together it looks like people are practically eatin' with folks they don't even know. It's mostly Black militia men, of course. I look down the long line again, in attempt to count the people. I give up once I see people standin' all outside.

I spot Jaybird. I met her at the bar last night. We ended up having a great time in one of the private backrooms. I'm gonna see if we can do that again tonight. If only she could lose that gorilla lookin' pimp of hers. She said she's from Chicago and had to lie in order to get a passport to come here. I'm still wondering what lies she told and why? I'll certainly try to find out tonight. She said her boss thought being here was better because the Vietnam vets are willin' to pay more since they're away from their women. I would've been able to learn more about her had it not been for her gorilla interruptin' our conversation. Gettin' all in my fuckin' face talkin' about "time is money." If

I didn't have mad respect for the bar owner, I would've slammed his fat, ugly ass. I'm surprised he's not glued by her side now.

"You ready to order, sir?" The waitress interrupts my thoughts. I look her over and say, "Whoooa! So, you're Ms. Ling Ling, huh?"

"Yes," she replies.

"Well…uh…now I see the real reason it's mostly men flockin' in here." I scan her body from head to foot. "Woman if those blue jean Daisy Dukes were any smaller, they'd be invisible. I don't even need to order any food now. I've already gulped down dessert with my eyes." She smiles while shifting her weight to the opposite leg. "Okay…Imma stop meddlin withcha…I want Chitlins, hams, collards, dressin', mac and cheese, Black eyed peas and corn bread. And add an extra corn bread with that, please."

As she reaches for the menu she asks, "Would you like something to wash that down with?"

"Yes, I would." As I look her over, she fidgets with her writin' pad. "A Schlitz malt liquor beer…please and thanks." As she tries to take the menu out my hand, I get an idea and hold tight to it. She raises her eyebrows. "I'm gonna hold on to this for a few minutes." As I stand up, I let her know, "I'm stepping out but I'm comin' right back." I bend down, look her square in the eyes and say, "Ms. Ling Ling, don't give nobody my table now…ya hear." She giggles, nods and bounces away as her long black ponytail sways.

I squeeze my way between chairs, tables and people. I finally get outside and walk up to Jaybird. I ask her, "Hey Ms. Lady. Whatchu gonna eat?"

"Oh heeey! Not really sure yet. I wanted to look at the menu first," she replies, actually looking happy to see me.

"Well, I musta read yo mind, woman. Here ya go." I give her the menu.

Her eyes light up as she says, "Wow. Thank you."

I ask her, "You here alone?"

She rolls her eyes and says, "Ha! Like that'll ever happen aga…"

I wonder why she cut off her words. She buries her head in the menu. To ease the tension, but that doesn't stop me from messing with her. "So, did you go get that pregnancy test yet?"

Her head pops up for a few seconds, with a look of confusion and embarrassment. She smacks her lips, chuckling and looking back at the menu she says, "Please that aint happenin'."

"So whatchu gonna name him if it's a boy?" I continue teasing her

She doesn't look up from the menu this time and gets loud. "Man, you betta quit playin' wit' me!"

"Okay. Okay." I chuckle and wait a few seconds before changin' the subject. "So didchu decide whatchu wanna eat?"

"Yeah. I could go for some fried chicken, mustard and turnips, macaroni and cheese and yams," she says.

"Damn! Sounds like you really *are* eatin' fa two to me," I flash a lingering smile. "You're more than welcome to join me," I tell her.

She looks over at a parked car and says, "I really can't come in. I have to order to go."

"Tell you what…I'll place that order for you and by the time you get to the front of the line it should be ready. Or I can just brang it out if it's done before that…Is that cool?"

She nods. I get ready to head back inside but turn around to glance in the direction where she looked in hopes of spotting which car the gorilla was sitting in. I don't see anyone. I ask her, "Will you be back at the lounge again tonight?"

"Most likely," she says.

"What time can I expect you?"

"Probably about 9."

I smile. "Cool, I'll see you then. I'm gonna put yo order in now."

"Thank you."

"The pleasure is all mine, baby girl."

I can see Ms. Ling Ling placing my food on my table as I head that way. I slide into my seat and ask her, "Can I get some hot sauce?" I flash my slickster grin at her as she grabs a bottle from the now empty table in front of me, and places it on my table. Lookin' like she was about to run but I stop her. "Wait! I need to place an order to go." I repeat Jaybird's order as she writes it down.

"Coming right up," she says.

I'm almost finished eatin' when Ms. Ling Ling brings me the tab and Jaybird's order. I gulp down the last bite then pay her with cash and tell her to keep the change. "I should've known that would get a sincere smile out of those stiff lips," I tell her. It even looked like her ponytail bounced higher as she strutted away.

Jaybird is finally indoors, but still standin' in line. She's talkin' to another lady who's standin' behind her, so I stand there a few minutes. As the lady keeps directin' her eyes toward me this finally gets Jaybird's attention to turn around in order to see what the lady is lookin' at. As I hold her order up in front of her, she leans back and smile, looking surprised, as if we hadn't talked about me orderin' her food earlier. I ask her, "You forgot about our conversation earlier or did you think I just wasn't gonna actually do it?"

She hesitates before answerin'. "Probably a little bit of both." She giggles.

I lean in toward her to whisper. "Well, I'm glad I could show you otherwise. Don't fake me out tonight, Ms. Jaybird?" She looks me up and down and says, "Oh I'll be there."

I look her over. "Girl you said that like you meant that. See ya tonight," I say. We both smile. I walk away as she turns back to the lady in line and continues talkin'.

The temperature has spiked to an egg-fryin'-on-the-concrete level of mugginess since this mornin', but this is typical for Saigon all year round though. I notice more vendors have set up shops closer to the restaurant now. Some food joints have tables and chairs set-up outdoors, so people are eatin' as they swat at bugs.

I wave at Papa Son. He wasn't out here earlier. Papa Son is what they call Vietnamese men. He done set up a bar out here. Booooi…they out here makin' that money.

I get to the crosswalk and notice a girl, who looks about ten years old, and over dressed for the weather. But what stands out more is she looks pregnant. Got me wonderin' if she a hooker too? It's so crowded I can barely get through all these people.

Just as I step off the curb there's an explosion so powerful it makes the ground shake. I instantly dive to the ground, wondering if it was an earthquake. People are screamin' and runnin' in every direction. I lift my head to see what's goin' on. People are lookin' and pointin' behind me. I turn to see a cloud of dark smoke. It's near the soul food restaurant. Rememberin' Jaybird, I jump up from the ground and run back toward the restaurant.

I slow down because it's difficult to see, but it's clear that er'thang is a heap of mess. The rooftops are now on the ground. I look down at what looks like an arm. Some people are walkin' around cryin', blood oozin' from various places on their bodies. Black soot is everywhere. Some have smoke comin' from their heads and clothes. I try lookin' in cars for Jaybird and her gorilla but I can't find them. Too many cars are now either turned sideways or upside down.

Sirens are approaching.

Useless Labels

"Thinking out loud."
What the flock does that really mean?
No one can actually *do* that.
It's still talking out loud.

"Talking to myself."
No, you're not if others are near and can hear you.

Both are horrendous phrases.

Include them with
Pointless
Unnecessary
Useless societal labels.

How about those "responsive intentions?"
More like non-responsive and failed to mention.
A thing was said or not but is now undoable.

That irrational comment festers days later.
Leaving you desiring to crush that fool like a worm under a jack hammer.
Wrecking their world for the endurance of their breathing lifespan!

You vow, "Next time...
Next time it's a cute little three-year-old
Appearing to not know any better.

But didn't she get that talk from an adult
who's shaping her absorbing brain?

Once again you ease back on using your cannonball phrases.
Only this time you're happy with yourself.

That adult you wanted to crush
is merely a former three-year-old
programmed on automated judgments.

Now the goal is to look at all as a three-year-old.
Instead of festering in anger have empathy.

You'll sleep well at night.
Even focus on more important issues
like what popping lipstick looks
better with that banging blouse!
You're now visualizing a female.

And
the
labeling
saga
continues…

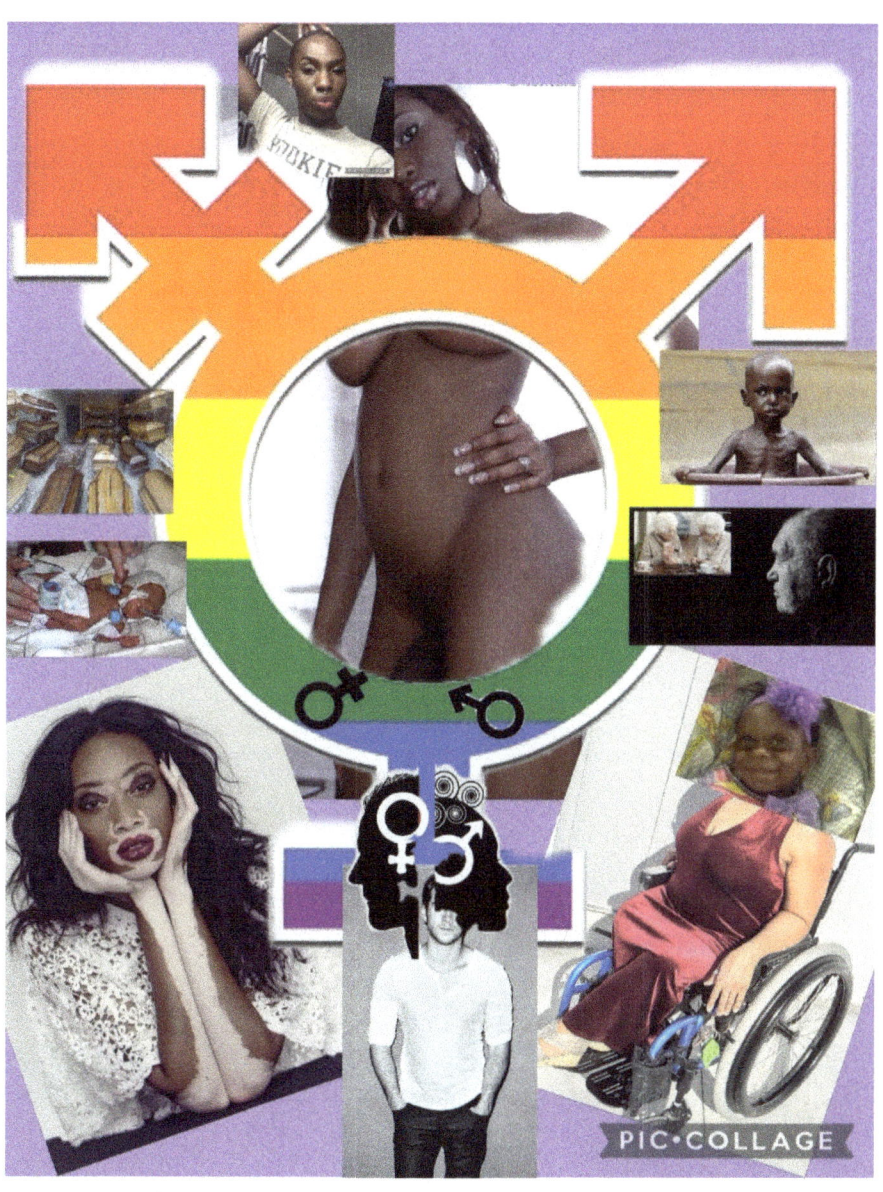

Turner-Tan the Estrogen Dom-i-nance

One hundred eighty-nine years ago
An arisen resurrection
Synonymous to erection
Autonomous to insurrection
Tearing down walls
For the American Negro

Sold, enslaved, raped, mistreated
Abolishing auras
Massive toxicity
Evil cultures defaced successfully
Former ways shall cease to be
Victimized and killed based on exterior pigment
Failed hopes of joyousness in life most gravid

Stifled and tortured
Still proclaiming civilized and virtuous masters
Unlike the doggish peasants of British Isles or Ireland
Certain people will never comprehend
Bound to free labor made to share borrowed land
The desire to still up rise and murder monarchs individually
Those honored as good ol' wholesome bastards

Southampton, Virginia is where I began
Know mo' justice know mo' peace
Interprets as no mo' justice and never no peace
Not requesting but demanding equality
It's born with you but rationed to me
Liberated solely for the human of being
Every continent globally is where I end

Labeled a dreadful conspiracy
By diabolical enslaved actors

Too long after the ship anchored
Way before being promised forty acres
Don't need a mule that's going to die
Like me…all for the sake of being free

Requiring a band of brutal miscreants
Under a new revolution
Though a temporary solution
Memorable throughout evolution
"Make America Great Again"
Via false accusations of *African Americans & Associates'* malfeasance

Stay Out the Funk

As much as we feel narcissists/psychopaths/sociopaths should want to change, although they are clearly not interested in doing so, it's just as difficult for us empaths to change, and obviously, we really do want to end codependency. The confusion for me is learning how to be this new person and remaining this way. I get annoyed with myself when I fall back into my old self like when my spirit gets low because that's the exact time when evil people, some who are complete strangers, feel comfortable with shytting on me. At first, I thought I must be sending out some sort of insecure vibes to those who love to kick people when they are down, but I noticed these people come out of the woodworks, even during my most confident and happy moments.

As of recently, I must say, I'm learning to speak up in my own subtle way and still be tactful about it, which is not what I would've done just years ago, so I'm patting myself on the back, feeling some progress. It feels good to not have to go home and either keep reliving the scene in my mind—ruminating as it's called—with what I should've said or telling anybody who would listen about how this shytty person attempted to make me feel inferior. Or worse, crying on my pillow due to pitying myself. I would replay the scene in my head of what they said and what I should've said or done. But then I found a Bible verse, which I can't even remember which one, and I'm consoled for the choice I made to not lash out. Oh yeah, it's "See that none render evil for evil unto any man; but ever follow that which is good, both among yourselves, and to all men." (1 Thessalonians)

I have had to deal with people trying to put me down all my life. I could just be quietly saying nothing to no one and there is always that one ignorant person trying to belittle me. At first, I couldn't understand it. People of various ages, different ethnicities and occupational status, would say ignorant stuff in front of others, or even sneakily to me, in attempt to belittle me. I was so distraught by it I wrote a poem and published it in *All Lives Matter* called "Ignorance Has No Age." But even it doesn't say enough to scratch the surface of describing the irritating menaces of evil doers.

Today, I now know that those people really feel like they are a nobody. They are intimidated by the anointing power of God within me. But of course, I was clueless about it for so long, until I was made aware of it. A pastor said, "Some people are anointed and don't even know it!" It hit me then. That man of God is speaking to me. Another wise man posted on Facebook something like "you are unsure of yourself even though others are intimidated by you." That truth filled message was also for me.

I finally see it all so clearly now. Everything that I have suffered was to strengthen me. My confidence level, my writing skills and even my speaking capabilities. We all seek our purpose in life because it is horrible feeling useless. Some know what they are meant to do very young. While others don't figure it out until later, sometimes much later. But, my God, when one finally recognizes their purpose, it is a phenomenal feeling!

ALL the suffering I endured in my life has brought me to a beautiful place. One of my favorite quotes from a powerful man of God goes as such, "I could not have produced the fruit without the frustration. God could not ferment my fruit without the frustration. God could not ferment my fruit into His wine for maximum potency without my willingness to relinquish it to His winepress...Instead of condemning you to a graveyard, which is what you may feel, God is planting you in richer soil for greater fruit." TD Jakes from the daily bible plan (https://www.bible.com/bible/1/1th.5.17.kjv)

My life went from resembling Job's to resembling Joseph's—biblical characters in the bible. I stayed sickly as a child. Then as an adult I lost loved ones consecutively for years due to divorce and deaths. I dealt with grief for so long my so-called relatives and friends began abandoning me. My world was torn apart. But I had to change my perspective and remember we are all on an individual journey. We came in this world alone and we're leaving here alone. I had to die spiritually in order to build a new life for myself. The Bible backs up this turmoil, which helped to aid in my progress. "Verily, verily, I say unto you, Except a corn of wheat fall into the ground and die, it abideth alone: but if it die, it bringeth forth much fruit."

There are so many people who are suffering from various situations. It hurts so badly it seems as if it's never going to get better. If this is you, please know, it really does get better. At times, the hurt was so unbearable physically and emotionally I wanted to die. But I'm glad I didn't. What got me through is believing that God is preparing me for better. Also reading and hearing other people's victorious stories, motivational books, and inspirational quotes instilled in me a positive belief that I must come out on top. I have to win at this game of life because too many people wished I would fail and hoped for my demise. I refuse to give them that satisfaction!

Whatever you are going through just know that you are not alone! I pray that what I have shared has encouraged you!

A Giant

I visualized a giant
I now know what that was about
Building a higher impenetrable self
Boundaries beyond belief
Yeeeah that giant stood tall
Looking and walking over Harlem and North Avenue
Scared myself at first
Because unlike Goliath I didn't know who I was preparing to beat
But I see I had to beat myself into knowing my worth
Beat out those who thought they should be included in my hard-earned works
Beat out those who thrived on my energy leaving me depleted
Beat out those who took and took and took and never gave
Beat out those who drained the life out my kindness, my giving nature, my humanness as a nurturer
It's like rolling dough through a kneader
What oozes out on the other side
Peace
Happiness
More Peace
Joy
Abundant Peace
Satisfaction with being my own company
Profuse Peace beyond my own understanding
It's no longer an internal argument
More like a revelation of who's worthy and who should be cut from my glorious present and future
All those painful moments served a great purpose for my greater good
It was a necessity to not only see who wouldn't, but who absolutely would
I love my life more than ever before!

The Root of Toxicity

    Many are abused as children and manipulated into believing that family and even their own lives are supposed to be chaotic and depressing, or worse, abuse and hurt is what love looks like. They then become adults, and subconsciously seek those same traits they believed was love within friendships and even in intimate relationships. Some children quickly realize that something is not right about an adult treating them poorly. Some don't figure it out until they're way into adulthood. Some of those abusers who were abused in childhood end up, either completely forgetting their horrendous childhood to protect their heart and health or repeating the abuse that was done to them—treating others nastily, committing child molestations, becoming a serial killer, etc. Or they end up committing suicide. So, it is safe to say that victims of abuse either remain victims with different abusers or become abusers themselves. But, in some cases, victims and abusers may eventually get help and learn how to deal with people who treat them as their childhood abusers did and go on to teach others how to handle and disengage from toxic behaviors.

    My point here is everyone internalizes childhood abuse differently. If you are a victim or if you are an abuser, may you become a thriving survivor and end the vicious cycle of victimhood and being an abuser. Best of all, if you are thriving from all of the above, may you help others learn how to help themselves and others. The generational curses must cease now but it begins with the narrative changing in the mind!

Taboo Sentiments

"If you could see yourself through my eyes…" is what the card read. It aroused a warmth within me. It felt so sincere, like it was embracing me. It made me feel secure, validated even. The rest of the card was *just* as heartfelt. But *that* is the *only* sentence I can recall.

That was the first time I could actually consider anyone else's kind mindset being interested in who I was. After reading those words I kept glancing at my reflection, wherever and whenever, expecting to see myself transformed into *someone stunning. Anyone who could NOT possibly reflect me.*

Mom never confirmed anything about me resembling that card. If I changed my hairstyle, wore a new outfit or tried something new with my makeup, I got either no response or a repetitious monologue, "That doesn't look right on you." Likewise, I didn't expect any kindness from my siblings either. The only time I saw anything even remotely similar to fondness from them is when someone outside the family talked badly about me to them. Then an actual fist fight was probable.

I'm pretty positive that if the sperm donor had hung around, he too would NOT have been as empathetic as that card. I came to this conclusion in July of 2017. I traveled alone, on a road trip from Chicago, heading down south. The reason I chose to do so is because, for weeks, a voice in my head kept telling me to go south—when I awakened in the morning and before going to sleep at night. I know it sounds crazy, but certain voices are not just the frivolous imagination. I knew I wanted to eventually move to a warmer climate, so I assumed the voice was leading me to a reasonable home, waiting for me to purchase it, and I just needed to find where. Of course, I had to stop along the way to sleep in Georgia and Florida. I kept driving and saw New Orleans, Louisiana. My first thought was, well I've never been there. But I didn't get the feeling that that was the next place to go. I continue looking when I see the overhead sign, where my sperm donor resided in Mobile, Alabama (my mom mentioned this information when I was younger). That's when it hit me to head there. It is here where I learned of many more family members, which included three sisters and a brother from other mothers (my mom most likely didn't know anything about that).

Labelling Saga | 75

Unfortunately, the sperm donor had already died five years prior. But the most amazing part to me is my mom had passed away in May of 2016, and my brother passed away in February 2017. Today, I'm continuously wondering whose voice was it that was leading me in this direction, especially since I had tried on several occasions, prior to their deaths, to locate my sperm donor, and failed.

I was told my sperm donor suffered from PTSD after fighting in the Vietnam War. I tried so hard to find out *everything* about him because I've constantly heard, "If you ask the right questions, you'll get the right answers." Was I not asking the right questions? Since my newfound siblings were not spilling enough, I visited with my new found uncles and aunts and cousins. I basically asked, "What was his personality like?"

Was he nice?
Was he mean?
…Somewhere in between?

I asked everyone I met who mingled with him, but no one had much to say about him. It was as if they were hiding something. I didn't press the issue because I figured sentiments were just as taboo here as they were where I resided.

You see, I didn't feel a need to ever know him, EVER, until I had a precious little baby girl of my own. I could not comprehend how could he *not* care about his own daughter. The more I analyzed the more I cried. Since he took care of his other children what was wrong with me?

So, I got my answer from words on a card, given to me by a close cousin. I was shocked to learn that there was actually any other way to even see me outside of my distorted belief's way.

My way consisted of lack.
Lack of love.
Lack of beauty.
Lack of belief in me.
Lack of intelligence.
Lack of high self-esteem.
Lack of anything beyond worthiness.
BUT I DARE NOT LACK SENTIMENT.
No way do I want to be anything remotely like those who brainwashed me into believing lies of lack.

That card empowered me into believing that I
could wear a different pair of eyes.
REMOVING ALL THE BLURRED LINES.
That card made me believe that I am beautiful, even with my lack of straight blond hair.
That card made me believe that I am lovable even with my unsightly surgical scars and my lack of a model sized body.
That card convinced me that my wide flat nose is unique and sits perfectly on my face despite its lack of pointiness.
That card made me realize that it is absolutely normal to love myself despite how others made me feel so hated, because I believed that hating myself was the best option for everyone, especially myself.
That card made me realize that putting myself first is not selfish at all but absolutely necessary.
That card helped me to realize that saying yes when I really wanted to say no would not hurt anyone's feelings except my own, especially since allowing myself to be *inauthentic* evokes severe resentment.
That card helped me to build boundaries, while believing that it really does not go against God's will, especially since no one even knows what God's will is.
TODAY I WEAR MY NEW PAIR OF EYES QUITE NICELY.
I can see clearly
that those foreign pair of eyes, which were forced upon me,
were merely judging my outer beauty,
or lack thereof.
WELL THAT WOULD EXPLAIN
WHY MY REFLECTION NEVER CHANGED.
I'm glad it didn't because now I know
I DO NOT need Permanently
Tattooed makeup,
Or a rib removed,
Or a boob implant,
Or bleached skin,
Or relaxed hair,
Or liposuction,
Or a nose job,

Labelling Saga

Or Botox,
 Or an ass injection.

I can, *finally*, see

that shattering generational curses

of believing that sentiments are taboo

is sincerely

A VERY MUCH NEEDED PHENOMENON!

The Horrids Prior

She said, "Divorce is like a death trap."
Wasn't even married yet
Did she share to vent
Or a premonition sent

When one thinks they're in love
The bad behaviors are shoved
Ignoring all the red flags
Forgiving those constant "my bads"

The lies caught, the disrespect
The discontinued loving texts
Date nights
Replaced with
Working late nights

Partner
Turned roommate
Turned ex mate
Turned ass-o-ciate

Why didn't she give the tea of the horrids before divorce
That part that leaves one no choice

Constant disagreements
For the sake of being hell bent

360 degrees is the new separation

Apart but never alone
Still living in the same home

Too terrified to leave
Claiming to remain for the babies

Less than frenemies
More like pretendies

Hate is seething
Neither being loving

Toleration lingers like a fed stray cat
Discomfort remains where hate lacks no slack

Attending functions with an upside-down smile
Inwardly fettered all the while

Posing & publicly posting portraits for the sake of it
Inner dialogue screaming, "This is some bullshyt!"

Mentality recanting "for better & worse"
Deeply eager to not be the one to die first!

Wordless Response Spoken

Born in reverse
Void of sound
Image of wonder
Intense feelings of being
Yet no where
Floating out and away
Clouds remain still
Circular life forms
Wordless oxygen
Intense sound
Purple board
No form
Gold and white
Neatly placed
Once a man
Twice a child
Rapid, quick breaths
Thoughts flash
Mute response spoken
Life forms nearby
To listen
Back to the galaxy
Of the unborn life
CAN'T BREATHE.

Wall-less Jails=Badass Females

/?/?/Abortion or prochoice
*
Similarities with different names
*
Resembling fraternal twins or even cloned flames
∞ ∞ ∞ ∞ ∞ ∞ ∞ ∞ ∞ ∞ ∞ ∞ ∞ ∞
The following eliminates
*
Forced choices from unprotected love mates
*
Up to twelve thousand in the United States
*
A yearly rate
*

Victims of rape
*

/!/!/They fought, scratched, screamed, cried to not procreate
*

Yet still chose to celebrate
*

New baby's born date
*

/?/?/You heard me say
*

/!/!/in the states which claims unifi-cation
*

/!/!/Averages 250,000 females of severe heartache
∞ ∞ ∞ ∞ ∞ ∞ ∞ ∞ ∞ ∞ ∞ ∞ ∞ ∞
That rib cage tightened yet remains
*

Effortless against brain bashing pain
∞ ∞ ∞ ∞ ∞ ∞ ∞ ∞ ∞ ∞ ∞ ∞ ∞ ∞
The esophagus a fortitude of mystifying cages
*

self-defecating bodily, spewing outrage
∞ ∞ ∞ ∞ ∞ ∞ ∞ ∞ ∞ ∞ ∞ ∞ ∞ ∞
Callous of the skull like iron squelching a truth flowing
*

Saying…no…thing – Seeing…no…thing
*

Arresting too many from *EVER* knowing
∞ ∞ ∞ ∞ ∞ ∞ ∞ ∞ ∞ ∞ ∞ ∞ ∞ ∞
Stitch those natural slits
*

Suffocate those lustful fits
*

Involuntarily ceasing to indulge in laughter
and countless other enjoyable shyt
∞ ∞ ∞ ∞ ∞ ∞ ∞ ∞ ∞ ∞ ∞ ∞ ∞ ∞

/!/!/Spineless—damn near mindless—perpetrator now—
but a victim-of-abuse too then type beast
/!/!/Bore and tore—bore and tore—bore and tore—bore and tore
/!/!/Bore and tore—bore and tore—bore and tore—bore and tore
/!/!/Bore and tore—bore and tore—bore and tore—bore and tore
/!/!/Bore and tore—bore and tore—bore and tore—bore and tore
/!/!/some more—and more—and more—and more—and even more

∞ ∞ ∞ ∞ ∞ ∞ ∞ ∞ ∞ ∞ ∞ ∞ ∞ ∞

/?/?//!/!/*I certainly hope you feel that*
*If you didn't then you likely skipped reading the repetitiveness
And that's okay too*

∞ ∞ ∞ ∞ ∞ ∞ ∞ ∞ ∞ ∞ ∞ ∞ ∞ ∞ ∞

A wall-less jail

*

assists in reorganizing a heaven in hell

*

Beautifully formed cells

*

reproduced with a cowardice and fleeting male

*

/!/!/Yet loved unconditionally by a B*A*D*A*S*S F*E*M*A*L*E

Nightmaricide

A winding bridge, submerging into water
Rickety excitement!

From my turquoise Oldsmobile Cutlass Supreme
A gorgeous view—rather serene
Resembling an amusement park without a theme
The speed accelerates, switching the scene
Pumping and pulling all brakes, I scream

Soundless shrieks, paralyzed sound
Up, then down, ceaselessly swirling around
My only desire: return to ground
Sinking underwater I'm finally down

Water fills the car, depleting all energies merely to fail
Yearning to say goodbye to family, fishing for my cell
Can't dial the number correctly in such a horrendous panic
I give up and succumb to whatever is next

Time, no longer on my side
                        I feel my soul slightly rise
                                              Nightmaricide!

               Peeeeeeees—enveeeeeeluuuuups—meeeeeeee

        I-------------------EMBRACE-------------------IT

               Ill concerned with who or what was
Exhilaration turned terror
      L E R
    L   C
 O   O
R   A
          S
           T
            E
             R
              R
              I
             D
            E
             ~~^~^~^~^~^~^~~~~~~^~~~~~^~~~~~~~~~~~~~
                                                 of horror!

OVERANALYZE

There are several ways to skin a cat.

I don't even like cats.

Therefore, I don't know no way of doing it.

Unless you can teach it to bark!

Versos 1

Did you even notice? Micti asks. There are literally millions of visible and invisible things surrounding us at this current moment.

Seeing that I can't nor have time to count that high why don't you just come right out & tell me what I should notice? Survi retorts.

*The bleeding Robots with Human DNA**. They're everywhere & you're absolutely correct about the invisible part because they come in all forms & will go out of their way to blend in.*

Versos 1.1

I love you.
Not sincerely.
Only in deeds.

Eventually those fades.

I don't mind helping really means I'll be back for my due soon.

I'm happy for your accomplishments.
Nah!
I'm jealous & will easily wreck your day, your life even, because you are unaware.
That is until you are.

Functioning vascular organs. Feeling nothing. They perceive & absorb conversations, mannerisms, & their personality permanence are funereal.

Some are covert. While others are overt, standing out like a gorgeously blossomed entourage of pink petals among green monotonous roughage. After they've been noticed they remain outside of themselves, at least to those who know the truth. Micti says.

You call me on my bullshyt. You'll pay for that. I don't like standing out. Sometimes I'll go to extremes to not. Other times I'll make me your god. Gaslighting. Triangulating. Hoovering. Calling & texting… incessantly. Abandoning. Then returning uninvited at your home, workplace, grocery store, fitness center, garage. Get you all comfortable again just to ghost you again when you least expect it again. Excessive & useless conversations & messages of feigned concern are my best ways in. I'll *say* something stupid today, but I'll *do* something stupid another day. Recruiting loyal flying monkeys. Helping to spread vicious gossip & lies against you. It's empowering to use your own blood relatives—my former in-laws—& even your childhood friends to help me phuk you over. It doesn't matter that you've gone gray rock, detached, or even no contact with them too. I'll stick around them for whatever useless reason & report back to you what I know just to remind you that you've been abandoned by everyone while I'm continuing to be that thorn in your side!

Pure conceptualism negates the need for loving in the traditional emotional sense. One does not need to love those Robots with Human DNA when it's merely based on the idea of love.

Metal Carcass

Surrounding sands and fog
Endless

A blurred dream
Boundless

A detached swamp of steel
Immeasurable

Blended and piled gravel and dirt
Incalculable

Windlessness
Firelessness
Resembles a new hell

Devoid of life
A new resting place for no one
A metal carcass

NOT Who We Want

Dear Mr. ▓▓▓▓shitz,

As much as I try to challenge myself to become more kinder today than I was yesterday, today I shall fail that challenge. Upon meditating on the seven contractors who've worked here there are only two who have done satisfactory work. Yours was not one! Allow me to disclose that the most times you've annoyed me to the core, during the months you were here is when you continued breathing.

I have taken valuable time out from my treasured schedule, per your request, to complete your survey. I only completed the numbers rating scale portion because I figured you'll know by the total number of zeros that I would never recommend ▓▓▓▓fuc Contractors to even ▓▓dent ▓▓ber ▓▓rty-▓▓ve or anyone as orange as him.

There's a saying, "You can tell a lot by the size of a man's feet." So, I'm just curious, does it bother you to have to walk around with a ▓▓▓▓dik your entire life? I can't help but to ponder if your mother had eaten you prior to cutting the umbilical cord… You know what never mind I respect mama ▓▓▓▓shitz too much to wish that type of indigestive pain, akin to digesting bricks, on her that way.

But I must confess the one time you actually made me happy was when you finally had no reason to return. The most pleasant thing I could say in ending this letter is if despair was a person, you would be it! And it sincerely hurts me to insult despair in this manner!

Love Mrs. B.I. ▓▓▓▓tch

We attract who we are not who we want.

We attract who we are not who we want.

We attract who we are not who we want.

We attract who we are not who we want.

We attract who we are not who we want.

We attract who we are not who we want.

We attract who we are not who we want.

We attract who we are not who we want.

We attract who we are not who we want.

Labelling Saga

Grasping Obliteration

Sinkholes
Distressing
Intermittently ingurgitating the least expectant
Nightmares of a crutch slipping underworld
Frightened
Scrunching to halt an entire gulp
Vainful attempts to cease
Falling
Endlessness
Infinite gargantuan murkiness
Horrified
Blinded by obsidian
Fear
Breathlessness
Grasping rapaciously toward obliteration
Petrified
Terror dissipates
Along with
Exhalation and Inhalation
Terrified
Until returning to light

All-Time Nothing

The thing arrives now	I'd answer…
not when developing	that is no…
the feel comes	But sometimes
am emerging there	silence is good
and seem a coincidence	and now is the time
	I'll know the time
whether we're not listening	though there is an answer
listen like we answer	something is physically ignored
	an all-time nothing than I
though just asking	to be fast enough I keep myself new
suppose some may not really ask	a question most frustrating is
	who I may want to be
exact answer is better	or mind not to be

Looming

the mind
that humungous foot
prepped to crush

        another woman
        some woman
        any woman

                that woman
                your own self
                dear woman

        intertwined
        constantly enduring
        together

                lingering
                in mid-air
                as if it grew there

creative/science fiction/fiction
wishful thinking
the equivalencies are frightening

        coveting to generate
        that which no one else
        has dared to make

                taking nothing
                producing something
                crushing all competitors

                        despite millions in opposition
                        writing, in mind
                        editing, incessantly

re-writing cerebrally
revising in dreams
correcting so hard it feels really real

      returning to monitor
      only to realize
      there are no such occurrences

            it starts
            all over again
            with enhancements

                  it never ceases
                  & I pray not
                  it's the only excitement I got

treading places
no one else dares
any and everywhere

      across continents
      between planets of doom
      within colons entertainments loom

            generating foreign places
            experiencing unique pains
            nothing will ever remain

                  conversing with characters
                  who didn't exist ten seconds ago
                  don't like 'em – let 'em go

              elating sensations
              inflating realisms
              swollen delusional empowerment

NO
  ONE

    &

     NO

      THING

       CAN

        HALT

         IT

          NOT

           EVEN

            I!

LAMERA

God blessed me with a beautiful daughter. Thank you Varrina for choosing me to be your mom. It is sincerely an honor and my pleasure to serve you. My only goal is for you to be happy. I pray that I've helped to make that happen. Life can be a good place or a rough place to reside. We choose which we want it to be. Your presence made my life happier. Nothing is more fulfilling than being at peace in the presence of the right people. You remained my peace. For that I am forever gratefully.

Life's
Adventurous,
Majestic
Eagles
Rise
Above

I chose your middle name, Lamera, because the derivative stems from miracle, which is exactly what you are to me. Your life keeps me motivated. It is because of you I maintained a desire to continue pressing on and being adventurous. Your presence helped me to desire royalty, to want to rise higher. Thank you for giving me a reason to continue believing in a kind humanity, that loving spirits still exist, for reminding me of my strength when I became weak. Thank you for being a continued blessing in my life. Thank you for being awesome! Please maintain that beauty within and without, no matter what life throws at you. I love you, baby!

My Grand Baby Girl

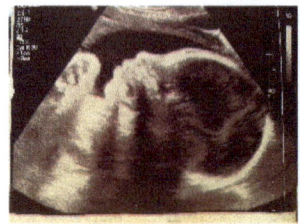   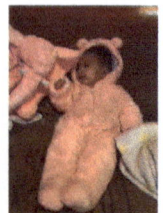

You beat with my heart
My precious grand baby girl
My name sake
Loving
Attitude &
Reliving
Introspectively
Solidifies
Selflessness
Always
It's amazing how being in love
Changes with each person
The day you popped out full of goo and blood
I couldn't stop gawking at another one of God's great creation
Rocking you on my chest
I wouldn't take nothing less
This quiet moment of just me and you
Feeling the weight of your relaxation ensue
Eyes slowly closing
Proud I helped with that
Continuing to gently rock
Desiring to remain this way eternally
Who needs to eat
Who needs sleep
Just want to keep rocking you so lovingly gently

Oh, by the way
I'm honored you took my name
I barely use it anyway
I love you baby doll!

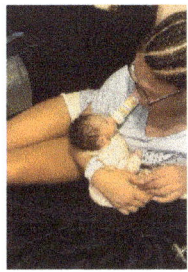

CHASE THE DRE-E-E-EAM

Chase the dre-e-e-eam Black Girls
It's you who needs to be se-e-e-en
Express just what you me-e-e-ean
Show up and make sce-e-e-enes
Your words are how you scre-e-e-eam
Your skin is the reason you ble-e-e-ed Black Girls
And a million more reasons to take he-e-e-ed
You were birthed in these worlds to le-e-e-ead
Only the ignorant will call you me-e-e-ean
Repeatedly-y-y-y
They expect you to disown your history-y-y-y Black Girls
Since you no longer bow down fearfully-y-y-y
Do you—just as you ple-e-e-ease
It's the real of how things should be-e-e-e
Certain type of people don't want you to succe-e-e-ed
Learn to care less about **other's** ne-e-e-eds Black Girls
Listen closely-y-y-y
As I ple-e-e-ead
Keep making yourself priority-y-y-y
Not selfishly-y-y-y but lovingly-y-y-y
You are the one we **all** ne-e-e-ed Black Girls
Eradicate the ifs ands or buts and just belie-e-e-eve
Your presence fulfills generously-y-y-y
It's your life to live not society-y-y-y's
Life's a natural process you'll soon se-e-e-e
You have what it takes so proce-e-e-ed
      Generationally-y-y-y
         Continuously-y-y-y
Emboldened in badass bravery-y-y-y
Allow *no other being* to deter your journey-y-y-y
     BLACK GIRLS!!!!

Varrina L. Sims

 **Codeblack Life.**

What does #FREEDOM mean to you?🥺

I'll tell you what FREEDOM is to me— NO FEAR!

Nina Simone

Freedom is No Fear

All of us are violent
Until intuition or someone talk us out of it
Or at least this should be the case
Anger motivates
Sadness and hatred binds freedom
Or releases it
Or neither
All most often equaling fear

Nina Simone said "freedom is no fear"
Still too many remain in bondage

Fear is subjective
Until it is a matter of life or death
Minus the restraints

Objectivity is moot
When the options are limited
It's either fright, fight or flight
Destroy or be destroyed
Kill or be killed

Riots
Protests
Uprising
phucking shyt up
Murder
All assist in diminishing fear
So why don't we do more of that shyt
Randomly
Without another death
Without another injustice
Without fear

Many of our pale ancestors fought
Current loves are still fearlessly fighting
But an overwhelming number let fear rule over them
Leaving millions of Bold Beautiful Black women and men
To fend for themselves
Continuing to
Bleed
Die
Shed tears
In hopes of easing our future fears

Billie Holiday beautifully sang
Expressions of "Strange Fruit"
Even after being incessantly stalked and harassed
By white men
Then set up
and thrown into the pen
Labeled another unruly Black Woman

Those who are not destroyed by outside rage
Begin raging against themselves
In hopes of bearing a better way
Dealing with the roaring rage
Only to end in a losing battle
Against inevitable rage

Raging against rage
Ragingly raging against rage
UNCONTROLLABLE RAGE

Shakespeare had it semi-correct
To comply or not to comply that is the real question
The murders of the Black and Brown
Meant to keep us in a disoriented place
Like guerrillas of warfare—confused, submissive, more fearful

Behave
Or even misbehave
In order to break free
From that fearful mentality
Of modern-day slavery
The end result is murder
Bullet or broken heart

Breathing
Means global continental & continual rape
Of liberty
Of freedom
Of independence
Of autonomy
Of air
Of breath
Of regenerating organisms

I CAN'T BREATHE
No longer equals an ending of life
But the end of living

What will it take
Intermixing each and every race
Deceiving the eyes of prejudices
Leaving them befuddled
Without a hate to stand on
When they ask
What are you
Don't answer
Whose turn is it next
To fight for fearlessness

Predecessors took the beatings and killings
Now rest snuggly in their graves
In hopes that current generations can reap

Fearlessness and freedom
Yet nothing's changed

Descendants
Some day
You shall run into fewer issues
Free from senseless killings
No longer being extremely more cautious
Than our pale equals
Or walking on eggshells

Of course
Some day
Just not today
As we wait for another jury's verdict
Anticipating more mayhem and more murders
The Wall Street Journal headline states:
Awaiting Derek Chauvin Verdict, Police Prepare New Approach to Protests[1]

NO ONE
Should get injured or die during a routine traffic stop or unexpected arrest

When will it read:
A new approach in the police department for better training and less murders during arrests

The National Guards are also called in to prepare for crowd control
There is obviously not enough backlash from foreign enemies
Since they are now being used against our hopeful and fearless U.S. citizens!

This verdict is in!
At 1:44 PM on April 20, 2021

Derek Chauvin Found guilty on all three charges in the death of George Floyd!
Totally shocked! From the look on Derek's face, he is too.

Next is the sentencing
Whatever it is, it's still just another light tap on the hand
Too many other authoritarian guilties are still free
This feels like progress
As it continues being a short term
Temporary solution
To a long-term permanent bondage!

> *It pains me to think that once this book is finally published*
> *too many more minorities' names will need to be added to this list.*
> *I shudder at the thought that those Black Women*
> *who were murdered in my hometown*
> *could have been either my daughter, granddaughter or even me.*
> *The following list is consecrated.*
> *It is because of their deaths so many other lives were spared.*
> *God, I pray continued protection for all.*

Daunte Demetrius Wright, October 27, 2000 - April 11, 2021[2]
Brooklyn Center, Minnesota
Shot: Brooklyn Center Police Officer, April 11, 2021

Marvin David Scott III, 1995 - March 14, 2021
McKinney, Texas
Peppered sprayed/Restrained with spit hood/Asphyxiated: 7 Collin County Jail Detention Officers, March 14, 2021

Patrick Lynn Warren Sr., October 7, 1968 - January 10, 2021
Killeen, Texas
Shot: Killeen Police Officer, January 10, 2021

Vincent "Vinny" M. Belmonte, September 14, 2001 - January 5, 2021
Cleveland, Ohio
Shot: Cleveland Police Officer, January 5, 20201

Angelo Quinto, March 10, 1990 - December 26, 2020
Antioch, California
Knee on neck/Asphyxiated: December 23, 2020

Andre Maurice Hill, May 23, 1973 - December 22, 2020
Columbus, Ohio
Shot: December 22, 2020, Columbus Police Officer

Casey Christopher Goodson Jr., January 30, 1997 - December 4, 2020
Columbus, Ohio
Shot: December 4, 2020, Franklin County Sheriff Deputy

Angelo "AJ" Crooms, May 15, 2004 - November 13, 2020
Cocoa, Florida
Shot: November 13, 2020, Brevard County Sheriff Deputies

Sincere Pierce, April 2, 2002 - November 13, 2020
Cocoa, Florida
Shot: November 13, 2020, Brevard County Sheriff Deputies

Marcellis Stinnette, June 17, 2001 - October 20, 2020
Waukegan, Illinois
Shot: October 20, 2020, Waukegan Police Officer

Jonathan Dwayne Price, November 3, 1988 - October 3, 2020
Wolfe City, Texas
Tasered/Shot: October 3, 2020, Wolfe City Police Officer

Dijon Durand Kizzee, February 5, 1991 - August 31, 2020
Los Angeles, California
Shot: August 21, 2020, Los Angeles County Police

Rayshard Brooks, January 31, 1993 - June 12, 2020
Atlanta, Georgia
Shot: June 12, 2020, Atlanta Police Officer

Carlos Carson, May 16, 1984 - June 6, 2020
Tulsa, Oklahoma
Pepper Sprayed/Shot in Head: June 6, 2020, Knights Inn Tulsa Armed Security Guard, former sergeant and detention officer with the Tulsa County Sheriff's Office

David McAtee, August 3, 1966 - June 1, 2020
Louisville, Kentucky
Shot: June 1, 2020, Louisville Metropolitan Police Officer

Tony "Tony the TIger" McDade, 1982 - May 27, 2020
Tallahassee, Florida
Shot: May 27, 2020, Tallahassee Police Officers

George Perry Floyd, October 14, 1973 - May 25, 2020
Powderhorn, Minneapolis, Minnesota
Knee on neck/Asphyxiated: May 25, 2020, Minneapolis Police Officer

Dreasjon "Sean" Reed, 1999 - May 6, 2020
Indianapolis, Indiana
Shot: May 6, 2020, Unidentified Indianapolis Metropolitan Police Officer

Michael Brent Charles Ramos, January 1, 1978 - April 24, 2020
Austin, Texas
Shot: April 24, 2020, Austin Police Detectives

Daniel T. Prude, September 20, 1978 - March 30, 2020
Rochester, New York
Asphyxiation: March 23, 2020, Rochester Police Officers

Breonna Taylor, June 5, 1993 - March 13, 2020
Louisville, Kentucky
Shot: March 13, 2020, Louisville Metro Police Officers

Manuel "Mannie" Elijah Ellis, August 28, 1986 - March 3, 2020
Tacoma, Washington
Physical restraint/Hypoxia: March 3, 2020, Tacoma Police Officers

William Howard Green, March 16, 1976 - January 27, 2020
Temple Hills, Maryland
Shot: January 27, 2020, Prince George's County Police Officer

John Elliot Neville, 1962 - December 4, 2019
Winston-Salem, North Carolina
Asphyxiated (hog-tied in prone position)/Heart Attack/Brain Injury: December 2, 2019, Forsyth County Sheriff Officers

Atatiana Koquice Jefferson, November 28, 1990 - October 12, 2019
Fort Worth, Texas
Shot: October 12, 2019, Fort Worth Police Officer

Elijah McClain, February 25, 1996 - August 30, 2019
Aurora, Colorado
Chokehold/Ketamine/Heart Attack: August 24, 2019, Aurora Police Officers and Paramedic

Ronald Greene, September 28, 1969 - May 10, 2019
Monroe, Louisiana
Stun gun/Force: May 10, 2019, Louisiana State Police

Javier Ambler, October 7, 1978 - March 28, 2019
Austin, Texas
Tasered/Electrocuted: March 28, 2019, Williamson County Sheriff Deputy

Sterling Lapree Higgins, October 27, 1981 - March 25, 2019
Union City, Tennessee
Choke hold/Asphyxiation: March 24-25, 2019, Union City Police Officer and Obion County Sheriff Deputies

Gregory Lloyd Edwards, September 23, 1980 - December 10, 2018
Brevard County Jail, Cocoa, Florida
Kneed, Punched, Pepper Sprayed, Tasered, and Strapped into a restraint chair with a spit hood over his head/Failure to Provide Medical Care: December 9, 2019, Brevard County Sheriffs

Emantic "EJ" Fitzgerald Bradford Jr., June 18, 1997 - November 22, 2018
Hoover, Alabama
Shot: November 22, 2018, Unidentified Hoover Police Officers

Charles "Chop" Roundtree Jr., September 5, 2000 - October 17, 2018
San Antonio, Texas
Shot: October 17, 2018, San Antonio Police Officer

Chinedu Okobi, February 13, 1982 - October 3, 2018
Millbrae, California
Tasered/Electrocuted: October 3, 2018, San Mateo County Sheriff Sergeant and Sheriff Deputies

Anton Milbert LaRue Black, October 18, 1998 - September 15, 2018
Greensboro, Maryland
Tasered/Sudden Cardiac Arrest: September 15, 2018, Greensboro Police Officers

Botham Shem Jean, September 29, 1991 - September 6, 2018
Dallas, Texas
Shot: September 6, 2018, Dallas Police Officer

Antwon Rose Jr., July 12, 2000 - June 19, 2018
East Pittsburgh, Pennsylvania
Shot: June 19, 2018, East Pittsburgh Police Officer

Saheed Vassell, December 22, 1983 - April 4, 2018
Brooklyn, New York City, New York
Shot: April 4, 2018, Four Unnamed New York City Police Officers

Stephon Alonzo Clark, August 10, 1995 - March 18, 2018
Sacramento, California
Shot: March 18, 2018, Sacramento Police Officers

Dennis Plowden Jr., 1992 - December 28, 2017
East Germantown, Philadelphia, Pennsylvania
Shot: December 27, 2017, Philadelphia Police Officer

Bijan Ghaisar, September 4, 1992 - November 27, 2017
George Washington Memorial Parkway, Alexandria, Virginia
Shot: November 17, 2017, U.S. Park Police Officers

Aaron Bailey, 1972 - June 29, 2017
Indianapolis, Indiana
Shot: June 29, 2017, Indianapolis Metropolitan Police Officers

Charleena Chavon Lyles, April 24, 1987 - June 18, 2017
Seattle, Washington
Shot: June 18, 2017, Seattle Police Officers

Fetus of Charleena Chavon Lyles (14-15 weeks), June 18, 2017
Seattle, Washington
Shot: June 18, 2017, Seattle Police Officers

Jordan Edwards, October 25, 2001 - April 29, 2017
Balch Springs, Texas
Shot: April 29, 2017, Balch Springs Officer

Chad Robertson, 1992 - February 15, 2017
Chicago, Illinois
Shot: February 8, 2017, Chicago Police Officer

Deborah Danner, September 25, 1950 - October 18, 2016
The Bronx, New York City, New York
Shot: October 18, 2016, New York City Police Officers

Alfred Olango, July 29, 1978 - September 27, 2016
El Cajon, California
Shot: September 27, 2016, El Cajon Police Officers

Terence Crutcher, August 16, 1976 - September 16, 2016
Tulsa, Oklahoma
Shot: September 16, 2016, Tulsa Police Officer

Terrence LeDell Sterling, July 31, 1985 - September 11, 2016
Washington, DC
Shot: September 11, 2016, Washington Metropolitan Police Officer

Korryn Gaines, August 24, 1993 - August 1, 2016
Randallstown, Maryland
Shot: August 1, 2016, Baltimore County Police

Joseph Curtis Mann, 1966 - July 11, 2016
Sacramento, California
Shot: July 11, 2016, Sacramento Police Officers

Philando Castile, July 16, 1983 - July 6, 2016
Falcon Heights, Minnesota
Shot: July 6, 2016, St. Anthony Police Officer

Alton Sterling, June 14, 1979 - July 5, 2016
Baton Rouge, Louisiana
Shot: July 5, 2016, Baton Rouge Police Officers

Bettie "Betty Boo" Jones, 1960 - December 26, 2015
Chicago, Illinois
Shot: December 26, 2015, Chicago Police Officer

Quintonio LeGrier, April 29, 1996 - December 26, 2015
Chicago, Illinois
Shot: December 26, 2015, Chicago Police Officer

Corey Lamar Jones, February 3, 1984 - October 18, 2015
Palm Beach Gardens, Florida
Shot: October 18, 2015, Palm Beach Gardens Police Officer

Jamar O'Neal Clark, May 3, 1991 - November 16, 2015
Minneapolis, Minnesota
Shot: November 15, 2015, Minneapolis Police Officers

Jeremy "Bam Bam" McDole, 1987 - September 23, 2015
Wilmington, Delaware
Shot: September 23, 2015, Wilmington Police Officers

India Kager, June 9, 1988 - September 5, 2015
Virginia Beach, Virginia
Shot: September 5, 2015, Virginia Beach Police Officers

Samuel Vincent DuBose, March 12, 1972 - July 19, 2015
Cincinnati, Ohio
Shot: July 19, 2015, University of Cincinnati Police Officer

Sandra Bland, February 7, 1987 - July 13, 2015
Waller County, Texas
Excessive Force/Wrongful Death/Suicide (?): July 10, 2015, Texas State Trooper

Brendon K. Glenn, 1986 - May 5, 2015
Venice, California
Shot: May 5, 2015, Los Angeles Police Officer

Freddie Carlos Gray Jr., August 16, 1989 - April 19, 2015
Baltimore, Maryland
Brute Force/Spinal Injuries: April 12, 2015, Baltimore City Police Officers

Walter Lamar Scott, February 9, 1965 - April 4, 2015
North Charleston, South Carolina
Shot: April 4, 2015, North Charleston Police Officer

Eric Courtney Harris, October 10, 1971 - April 2, 2015
Tulsa, Oklahoma
Shot: April 2, 2015, Tulsa County Reserve Deputy

Phillip Gregory White, 1982 - March 31, 2015
Vineland, New Jersey
K-9 Mauling/Respiratory distress: March 31, 2015, Vineland Police Officers

Mya Shawatza Hall, December 5, 1987 - March 30, 2015
Fort Meade, Maryland
Shot: March 30, 2015, National Security Agency Police Officers

Meagan Hockaday, August 27, 1988 - March 28, 2015
Oxnard, California
Shot: March 28, 2015, Oxnard Police Officer

Tony Terrell Robinson, Jr., October 18, 1995 - March 6, 2015
Madison, Wisconsin
Shot: March 6, 2015, Madison Police Officer

Janisha Fonville, March 3, 1994 - February 18 2015
Charlotte, North Carolina
Shot: February 18, 2015, Charlotte-Mecklenburg Police Officer

Natasha McKenna, January 9, 1978 - February 8, 2015
Fairfax County, Virginia
Tasered/Cardiac Arrest: February 3, 2015, Fairfax County Sheriff Deputies

Jerame C. Reid, June 8, 1978 - December 30, 2014
Bridgeton, New Jersey
Shot: December 30, 2014, Bridgeton Police Officer

Rumain Brisbon, November 24, 1980 - December 2, 2014
Phoenix, Arizona
Shot: December 2, 2014, Phoenix Police Officer

Tamir Rice, June 15, 2002 - November 22, 2014
Cleveland, Ohio
Shot: November 22, 2014, Cleveland Police Officer

Akai Kareem Gurley, November 12, 1986 - November 20, 2014
Brooklyn, New York City, New York
Shot: November 20, 2014, New York City Police Officer

Tanisha N. Anderson, January 22, 1977 - November 13, 2014
Cleveland, Ohio
Physically Restrained/Brute Force: November 13, 2014, Cleveland Police Officers

Dante Parker, August 14, 1977 - August 12, 2014
Victorville, California
Tasered/Excessive Force: August 12, 2014, San Bernardino County Sheriff Deputies

Ezell Ford, October 14, 1988 - August 11, 2014
Florence, Los Angeles, California
Shot: August 11, 2014, Los Angeles Police Officers

Michael Brown Jr., May 20, 1996 - August 9, 2014
Ferguson, Missouri
Shot: August 9, 2014, Ferguson Police Officer

John Crawford III, July 29, 1992 - August 5, 2014
Beavercreek, Ohio
Shot: August 5, 2014, Beavercreek Police Officer

Tyree Woodson, July 8, 1976 - August 2, 2014
Baltimore, Maryland
Shot: August 2, 2014, Baltimore City Police Officer

Eric Garner, September 15, 1970 - July 17, 2014
Staten Island, New York
Choke hold/Suffocated: July 17, 2014, New York City Police Officer

Dontre Hamilton, January 20, 1983 - April 30, 2014
Milwaukee, Wisconsin
Shot: April 30, 2014, Milwaukee Police Officer

Victor White III, September 11, 1991 - March 3, 2014
New Iberia, Louisiana
Shot: March 2, 2014, Iberia Parish Sheriff Deputy

Gabriella Monique Nevarez, November 25, 1991 - March 2, 2014
Citrus Heights, California
Shot: March 2, 2014, Citrus Heights Police Officers

Yvette Smith, December 18, 1966 - February 16, 2014
Bastrop County, Texas
Shot: February 16, 2014, Bastrop County Sheriff Deputy

McKenzie J. Cochran, August 25, 1988 - January 29, 2014
Southfield, Michigan
Pepper Sprayed/Compression Asphyxiation: January 28, 2014, Northland Mall Security Guards

Jordan Baker, 1988 - January 16, 2014
Houston, Texas
Shot: January 16, 2014, Off-duty Houston Police Officer

Andy Lopez, June 2, 2000 - October 22, 2013
Santa Rosa, California
Shot: October 22, 2013, Sonoma County Sheriff Deputy

Miriam Iris Carey, August 12, 1979 - October 3, 2013
Washington, DC
Shot 26 times: October 3, 2013, U. S. Secret Service Officer

Barrington "BJ" Williams, 1988 - September 17, 2013
New York City, New York
Neglect/Disdain/Asthma Attack: September 17, 2013, New York City Police Officers

Jonathan Ferrell, October 11, 1989 - September 14, 2013
Charlotte, North Carolina
Shot: September 14, 2013, Charlotte-Mecklenburg Police Officer

Carlos Alcis, 1970 - August 15, 2013
Brooklyn, New York City
Heart Attack/Neglect: August 15, 2013, New York City Police Officers

Larry Eugene Jackson Jr., November 29, 1980 - July 26, 2013
Austin, Texas
Shot: July 26, 2013, Austin Police Detective

Kyam Livingston, July 29, 1975 - July 21, 2013
New York City, New York
Neglect/Ignored pleas for help: July 20-21, 2013, New York City Police Officers

Clinton R. Allen, September 26, 1987 - March 10, 2013
Dallas, Texas
Tasered and Shot: March 10, 2013, Dallas Police Officer

Kimani "KiKi" Gray, October 19, 1996 - March 9, 2013
Brooklyn, New York City, New York
Shot: March 9, 2013, New York Police Officers

Kayla Moore, April 17, 1971 - February 13, 2013
Berkeley, California
Restrained face-down prone: February 12, 2013, Berkeley Police Officers

Jamaal Moore Sr., 1989 - December 15, 2012
Chicago, Illinois
Shot: December 15, 2012, Chicago Police Officer

Johnnie Kamahi Warren, February 26, 1968 - February 13, 2012
Dothan, Alabama
Tasered/Electrocuted: December 10, 2012, Houston County (AL) Sheriff Deputy

Shelly Marie Frey, April 21, 1985 - December 6, 2012
Houston, Texas
Shot: December 6, 2012, Off-duty Harris County Sheriff's Deputy

Darnisha Diana Harris, December 11, 1996 - December 2, 2012
Breaux Bridge, Louisiana
Shot: December 2, 2012, Breaux Bridge Police Office

Timothy Russell, December 9. 1968 - November 29, 2012
Cleveland, Ohio
137 Rounds/Shot 23 times: November 29, 2012, Cleveland Police Officers

Malissa Williams, June 20, 1982 - November 29, 2012
Cleveland, Ohio
137 Rounds/Shot 24 times: November 29, 2012, Cleveland Police Officers

Noel Palanco, November 28, 1989 - October 4, 2012
Queens, New York City, New York
Shot: October 4, 2012, New York City Police Officers

Reynaldo Cuevas, January 6, 1992 - September 7, 2012
Bronx, New York City, New York
Shot: September 7, 2012, New York City Police Officer

Chavis Carter, 1991 - July 28, 2012
Jonesboro, Arkansas
Shot: July 28, 2012, Jonesboro Police Officer

Alesia Thomas, June 1, 1977 - July 22, 2012
Los Angeles, California
Brutal Force/Beaten: July 22, 2012, Los Angeles Police Officers

Shantel Davis, May 26, 1989 - June 14, 2012
New York City, New York
Shot: June 14, 2012, New York City Police Officer

Sharmel T. Edwards, October 10, 1962 - April 21, 2012
Las Vegas, Nevada
Shot: April 21, 2012, Las Vegas Police Officers

Tamon Robinson, December 21, 1985 - April 18, 2012
Brooklyn, New York City, New York
Run over by police car: April 12, 2012, New York City Police Officers

Ervin Lee Jefferson, III, 1994 - March 24, 2012
Atlanta, Georgia
Shot: March 24, 2012, Shepperson Security & Escort Services Security Guards

Kendrec McDade, May 5, 1992 - March 24, 2012
Pasadena, California
Shot: March 24, 2012, Pasadena Police Officers

Rekia Boyd, November 5, 1989 - March 21, 2012
Chicago, Illinois
Shot: March 21, 2012, Off-duty Chicago Police Detective

Shereese Francis, 1982 - March 15, 2012
Queens, New York City, New York
Suffocated to death: March 15, 2012, New York City Police Officers

Jersey K. Green, June 17, 1974 - March 12, 2012
Aurora, Illinois
Tasered/Electrocuted: March 12, 2012, Aurora Police Officers

Wendell James Allen, December 19, 1991 - March 7, 2012
New Orleans, Louisiana
Shot: March 7, 2012, New Orleans Police Officer

Nehemiah Lazar Dillard, July 29, 1982 - March 5, 2012
Gainesville, Florida
Tasered/Electrocuted: March 5, 2012, Alachua County Sheriff Deputies

Dante' Lamar Price, July 18, 1986 - March 1, 2012
Dayton, Ohio
Shot: March 1, 2012, Ranger Security Guards

Raymond Luther Allen Jr., 1978 - February 29, 2012
Galveston, Texas
Tasered/Electrocuted: February 27, 2012, Galveston Police Officers

Manual Levi Loggins Jr., February 22, 1980 - February 7, 2012
San Clemente, Orange County, California
Shot: February 7, 2012, Orange County Sheriff Deputy

Ramarley Graham, April 12, 1993 - February 2, 2012
The Bronx, New York City, New York
Shot: February 2, 2012, New York City Police Officer

Kenneth Chamberlain Sr., April 12, 1943 - November 19, 2011
White Plains, New York
Tasered/Electrocuted/Shot: November 19, 2011, White Plains Police Officers

Alonzo Ashley, June 10, 1982 - July 18, 2011
Denver, Colorado
Tasered/Electrocuted: July 18, 2011, Denver Police Officers

Derek Williams, January 23, 1989 - July 6, 2011
Milwaukee, Wisconsin
Blunt Force/Respiratory distress: July 6, 2011, Milwaukee Police Officers

Raheim Brown, Jr., March 4, 1990 - January 22, 2011
Oakland, California
Shot: January 22, 2011, Oakland Unified School District Police

                              Reginald Doucet, June 3, 1985 - January 14, 2011
                                                   Los Angeles, California
                                  Shot: January 14, 2011, Los Angeles Police Officer

Derrick Jones, September 30, 1973 - November 8, 2010
Oakland, California
Shot: November 8, 2010, Oakland Police Officers

                        Danroy "DJ" Henry Jr., October 29, 1990 - October 17, 2010
                                                  Pleasantville, New York
                              Shot: October 17, 2020, Pleasantville Police Officer

Aiyana Mo'Nay Stanley-Jones, July 20, 2002 - May 16, 2010
Detroit, Michigan
Shot: May 16, 2010, Detroit Police Officer

                    Steven Eugene Washington, September 20, 1982 - March 20, 2010
                                                          Los Angeles, California
                                    Shot: March 20, 2010, Los Angeles County Police

Aaron Campbell, September 7, 1984 - January 29, 2010
Portland, Oregon
Shot: January 29, 2010, Portland Police Officer

                             Kiwane Carrington, July 14, 1994 - October 9, 2009
                                                     Champaign, Illinois
                               Shot: October 9, 2019, Champaign Police Officer

Victor Steen, November 11, 1991 - October 3, 2009
Pensacola, Florida
Tasered/Run over: October 3, 2009, Pensacola Police Officer

Shem Walker, March 18, 1960 - July 11, 2009
Brooklyn, New York
Shot: July 11, 2009, New York City Undercover C-94 Police Officer

Oscar Grant III, February 27, 1986 - January 1, 2009
Oakland, California
Shot: January 1, 2009, BART Police Officer

Tarika Wilson, October 30, 1981 - January 4, 2008
Lima, Ohio
Shot January 4, 2008, Lima Police Officer

DeAunta Terrel Farrow, September 7, 1994 - June 22, 2007
West Memphis, Arkansas
Shot: June 22, 2007, West Memphis (AR) Police Officer

Sean Bell, May 23, 1983 - November 25, 2006
Queens, New York City, New York
Shot: November 25, 2006, New York City Police Officers

Kathryn Johnston, June 26, 1914 - November 21, 2006
Atlanta, Georgia
Shot: November 21, 2006, Undercover Atlanta Police Officers

Ronald Curtis Madison, March 1, 1965 - September 4, 2005
Danziger Bridge, New Orleans, Louisiana
Shot: September 4, 2005, New Orleans Police Officers

James B. Brissette Jr., November 6, 1987 - September 4, 2005
Danziger Bridge, New Orleans, Louisiana
Shot: September 4, 2005, New Orleans Police Officers

Henry "Ace" Glover, October 2, 1973 - September 2, 2005
New Orleans, Louisiana
Shot: September 2, 2005, New Orleans Police Officers

Timothy Stansbury, Jr., November 16, 1984 - January 24, 2004
Brooklyn, New York City, New York
Shot: January 24, 2004, New York City Police Officer

Ousmane Zongo, 1960 - May 22, 2003
New York City, New York
Shot: May 22, 2003, New York City Police Officer

Alberta Spruill, 1946 - May 16, 2003
New York City, New York
Stun grenade thrown into her apartment led to a heart attack: May 16, 2003, New York City Police Officer

Kendra Sarie James, December 24, 1981 - May 5, 2003
Portland, Oregon
Shot: May 5, 2003, Portland Police Officer

Orlando Barlow, December 29, 1974 - February 28, 2003
Las Vegas, Nevada
Shot: February 28, 2003, Las Vegas Police Officer

Nelson Martinez Mendez, 1977 - August 8, 2001
Bellevue, Washington
Shot: August 8, 2001, Bellevue Police Officer

Timothy DeWayne Thomas Jr., July 25, 1981 - April 7, 2001
Cincinnati, Ohio
Shot: April 7, 2001, Cincinnati Police Patrolman

Ronald Beasley, 1964 - June 12, 2000
Dellwood, Missouri
Shot: June 12, 2000, Dellwood Police Officers

Earl Murray, 1964 - June 12, 2000
Dellwood, Missouri
Shot: June 12, 2000, Dellwood Police Officers

Patrick Moses Dorismond, February 28, 1974 - March 16, 2000
New York City, New York
Shot: March 16, 2000, New York City Police Officer

Prince Carmen Jones Jr., March 30, 1975 - September 1, 2000
Fairfax County, Virginia
Shot: September 1, 2000, Prince George's County Police Officer

Malcolm Ferguson, October 31, 1976 - March 1, 2000
The Bronx, New York City, New York
Shot: March 1, 2000, New York City Police Officer

LaTanya Haggerty, 1973 - June 4, 1999
Chicago, Illinois
Shot: June 4, 1999, Chicago Police Officer

Margaret LaVerne Mitchell, 1945 - May 21, 1999
Los Angeles, California
Shot: May 21, 1999, Los Angeles Police Officer

Amadou Diallo, September 2, 1975 - February 4, 1999
The Bronx, New York City, New York
Shot: February 4, 1999, New York City Police Officers

Tyisha Shenee Miller, March 9, 1979 - December 28, 1998
Riverside, California
Shot: December 28, 1998, Riverside Police Officers

Dannette "Strawberry" Daniels, January 25, 1966 - June 7, 1997
Newark, New Jersey
Shot: June 7, 1997, Newark Police Officer

Frankie Ann Perkins, 1960 - March 22, 1997
Chicago, Illinois
Brutal Force/Strangled: March 22, 1997, Chicago Police Officers

Nicholas Heyward Jr., August 26, 1981 - September 27, 1994
Brooklyn, New York City, New York
Shot: September 27, 1994, New York City Police Officer

Mary Mitchell, 1950 - November 3, 1991
The Bronx, New York City, New York
Shot: November 3, 1991, New York City Police Officer

Yvonne Smallwood, July 26, 1959 - December 9, 1987
New York City, New York
Severely beaten/Massive blood clot: December 3, New York City Police Officers

Eleanor Bumpers, August 22, 1918 - October 29, 1984
The Bronx, New York City, New York
Shot: October 29, 1984, New York City Police Officer

Michael Jerome Stewart, May 9, 1958 - September 28, 1983
New York City, New York
Brutal Force: September 15, 1983, New York City Transit Police

Eula Mae Love, August 8, 1939 - January 3, 1979
Los Angeles, California
Shot: January 3, 1979, Los Angeles County Police Officers

Arthur Miller Jr., 1943 - June 14, 1978
Brooklyn, New York City, New York
Chokehold/Strangled: June 14, 1978, New York City Police Officers

Randolph Evans, April 5, 1961 - November 25, 1976
Brooklyn, New York City, New York
Shot in head: November 25, 1976, New York City Police Officer

Barry Gene Evans, August 29, 1958 - February 10, 1976
Los Angeles, California
Shot: February 10, 1976, Los Angeles Police Officers

Rita Lloyd, November 2, 1956 - January 27, 1973
New York City, New York
Shot: January 27, 1973, New York City Police Officer

Henry Dumas, July 20, 1934 - May 23, 1968
Harlem, New York City, New York
Shot: May 23, 1968, New York City Transit Police Officer

This memorial is in honor of those unarmed black and brown people killed by the police, sheriff deputies, and security guards. The list is organized by the most recent incident of police brutality (David McAtee and George Perry Floyd) and then moves back in time. I have listed each person by their name; birth and death dates; the location of their death; the means of death, date of death, and name of the police department.

I culled the names from a variety of online sources including Black Lives Matter's protests; Wikipedia; Black Past; Dangerous Objects, a website run by Mercy Garriga, that investigates cases of excessive use of force and death by the police force; and Professors Cassandra Chaney and Ray V. Robertson's essay "Armed and Dangerous? An Examination of Fatal Shootings of Unarmed Black People by Police." I have included women from the #SaveHerName project because we often ignore the injustices and violence that black women experience from the police: police brutality is real for women as it is for men.

At the age of twenty-four, a friend introduced me to the radical and astonishingly beautiful poetry and writing of Henry Dumas. His poetry serves as the epitaph for this memorial; Dumas is the last entry on this list, shot by New York City Transit Police on May 23, 1968.

— Renée Ater, May 29, 2020
Bio — Renée Ater (reneeater.com)

Much appreciation to Renée Ater for creating this much needed list of the senseless murders of our Black and Brown brothers and sisters.

I want to address the controversy about those choosing to participate in Black-on-Black killings versus Police officers who willingly participate in killing unarmed Black and Brown men, women and children, directly and indirectly. Most senseless crimes occurring among Blacks is due to lack—lack of education, lack of life skills, lack of opportunities, lack of higher paying jobs, lack of various resources, lack of proper parenting, lack of affordable living conditions, etc. When ignorance, poverty, and an inflated ego are factors in anything, bad decisions are made. Oftentimes, it is the people who expect something for nothing who are willing to cause unnecessary harm to others. But how does one justify intentional killings by those who are in higher power, and supposedly lack nothing? It appears, *the lack of integrity and morals should also be included in the list of lacks, even though most are saying it is the lack of training. It is obviously beneficial to not believe while still believing. Those who believe they should be allowed to take anything, even though it does not belong to them, justify it by revealing their lack, creating excuses as to why they did it, but the justice department calls it motive. Then there are those who believe their white privilege means they can do what they want to minorities, without repercussions. Again, there are those who feel that their entitlement means they are allowed to do it. You can decide whatever the "it" is in this case by using an example of some incident where one person murdered another and wants to convince the world why it had to be done, even though it was not in self-defense, or that cell phone was not a gun, or even though their backs were turned, and they fell to the ground after the first bullet hit them, yet the murderer believed there was still a need to unload the gun on a limp body or continue pressing a knee in the neck for nearly nine minutes. It does not matter that it's all caught on camera. Regardless of if it was not the full video, the murderer, is still found not guilty. Those involved in legalized killings are let off free while in most cases of Black-on-Black crime the murderer is usually **never** found. Murdered victims, and their loved ones, are given the unspoken message, to just get over it and move on. When I first started writing this, my intention was to give a reason why legalized killings are worse than Black-on-Black killings. But there is no such thing as a "worse murder." While murder is horrible to many there are obviously some who feel it's a necessity and needs to be done for the greater good. Although many may have faith in our judicial system, and everyone should expect more from them, this will never happen, if there continues to be souls who lack—integrity, morals, empathy, and love—and believe that their beliefs reign over all others, no matter what.*

Marvina Sims

1 [Awaiting Derek Chauvin Verdict, Police Prepare New Approach to Protests (msn.com)](#)

2 [https://www.reneeater.com/on-monuments-blog/tag/list+of+unarmed+black+people+killed+by+police](#)

BILLIE HOLIDAY

ANTHONY TREMMAGLIA FOR READER'S DIGEST

Wallow

Why do the spirits even attempt to warn me
It can't possibly be to soften the blow
My dream portrayed my brother leaving with a television in tow
I felt a premonition that he was packing up and getting ready to go

He ate in front of-
Always purchased the latest model of-
Basically, lived to sit in front of-
>That tv

Laughing at the same old jokes told by Sanford and his son
The bigoted and racist antics of old Archie Bunker tickled him as though they weren't even reruns
TV was his means to a world away from a mean world

So, when I saw him hauling that tv
I panicked
As if he reached into my chest
Controlling my erratic heartbeat
Inviting me deeper into dangers of the unmentionable
Many first ever foreign feelings
Unidentifiable grief stirred in profound despair

Continuously questioning him
Abundance of nervous and nerve wrecking anxiety
Asking repeatedly "why are you taking the tv!"
Why did I care so much
It didn't belong to me

It was the feeling of unwarranted fear that really concerned me
I could care less about that damned tv
I knew way deep down my brother was leaving
Taking himself out

Even in the dream
It was something to hide
Just like in real life
He held and hid it inside
Dropping subtle hints
How a crematory would suffice
Making it appealing to loved ones
Stressing it's the cheapest price

Getting reassurance that that one person wouldn't turn his death into a wave of gawkers
There were a few of us though
Staring at the hole in real-time as if it were a reality tv show

How come we never see them preparing to check out
Until way after hindsight
Like bro it's too late now since you've taken flight
Leaving us all behind to pounder how did we lose this fight
Could I have possibly altered his thoughts with mere words
Like would I have even had the nerve
to ask
Are you considering suicide
I suspect he would've gone into a ranting fit
Leaving me stuck on stupid like I'm the actual cray cray

That feeling in my dream explains a lot more than I'd actually know
He kept saying he would do it for so many years you know
It was when he stopped saying it that the bravery finally released its flow
That's why it's utterly important to watch and listen intently
For those things our loved ones would never show

A few of the worse things for me
is to wallow in regret, guilt, and insecurity

Years after you came to me in several dreams
I usually look them up to see what they mean

But this time they were quite clear
Reminding me you're no longer here
You chased me showing your fangs
Your unkempt hair flying everywhere
Overwhelming me with severe fear

The second crushed me with *your* feelings of despair
Now I understand why you wanted to be instantly out of here

Then finally you were calmly standing inside my home
turning away a peeping Tom
This loving gesture subdued me with much needed peace
Reminiscing on those days you made sure to protect me
Allowing me to put those hurtful moments well behind
Like dropping a heavy bag after carrying throughout time

Residual pain remains lingering off and on
Battling with the inner healing I've done for so long
As of today, I'm freer and can finally move on

Bore-dum Should No Longer Be a Cryme!

"One Saturday Morning"
Resembles the binge-watching theme song
Since the sixties
Hours of cartoons
That *only* adults find funny
My "go to" as I remain in place
Transforming my face
    Tasmanian Devil
    Woody Woodpecker
    Richie Rich
    Bam-Bam on the Flintstones
Until roughly noon

After that anything en-soos
Myst-eerie-cheerfulness
Morphs into my bff
Bore-dum
Someone else's worst nightmare

Unlike the average kid
Redundantly pretending with the same ole toys
Or models thereof
Or what's left of its
De-crep-it-ness
Gotta make my day more funner
By phu-ken sum shyt up!

Whatever is toss-ible
Goes straight out the 5th flo windo'
    Raw eggs
    Water balloons
    Batteries
    Kolorful golf ball sized klay-doe,

    Somebody's favorite shirt flows away like a deflated air balloon
    Fee-sees burning in a brown paper bag
Departing with massive other shyt I'll someday wish I still had

I look down to admire my genius
Only to stare into another pair
Glair-ring directly at me
A neighbor appalled
By my sess-pul of bee-u-tee-ful artistic fuc-her-ee

When life is the happiest
People yearn to invade
Police standing in the doorway
I wish their presence would fade
Impinging upon my and their own time
Bore-dum should no longer be a cryme!

Soren Kierkegaard

Everyone needs a little help sometimes.

Suicide:
CALL: 1-800-273-8255
OR
TEXT: HELLO TO 741741

Bullying:
1-800-420-1479
OR
TEXT: HOME TO 741741

Domestic Violence:
CALL: 1-800-799-7233
OR
TEXT: SUPPORT TO 741741

Self Harm:
CALL: 1-800-366-8288
OR
TEXT: CONNECT TO 741741

Sexual Assault:
CALL: 1-800-656-4673
OR
TEXT: HOME TO 741741

LGBTQ+:
CALL: 1-866-488-7386
OR
TEXT: START TO 678678

Abortion:
CALL: 1-866-439-4253
OR
TEXT: HELPLINE TO 313131

Pregnancy Infant & Child Loss:
CALL: 1-800-944-4773
OR
TEXT: HELLO TO 741741

Grief:
CALL: 1-800-445-4808
OR
TEXT: CARE TO 839863

Eating Disorders:
CALL: 1-800-931-2237
OR
TEXT: NEDA TO 741741

For more hotlines & resources visit:
GRIEFRESOURCENETWORK.COM

Mental Health:
CALL: 1-800-950-6264
OR
TEXT: NAMI TO 741741

Images used: The collage was created with Pic Collage. All portraits are either personal, or copied from Facebook, Google, and various websites.

www.ingramcontent.com/pod-product-compliance
Lightning Source LLC
Chambersburg PA
CBHW061201070526
44579CB00009B/87